# The Great Pyramid:
## A Factory for Mono-Atomic Gold

Spencer L. Cross

# DEDICATION

This ongoing work is but a piece of a much larger puzzle for humanity to coalesce, so we can understand our past and yet lunge forward together into freedom and peace.

This book is truly dedicated to my loving wife and beautiful children. Without their love, patience and understanding this whole idea would be floating in the ether waiting to be brought forth by another.

Together, we are children of light, equal and of one breath.

# CONTENTS

# ACKNOWLEDGMENTS

I would like to offer a special thank you to S. Jason Cunningham for being the soul in the fog walking along side of me as we march for truth.
The final push is underway.

Thank you, Ana, for encouraging me to speak.

Thank you Jerry for unlocking doors at the right moments.

Thank you Nancy for nudging me into the role of the teacher.

Thank you Kim for your last minute efforts!

Thank you CRK.

# INTRODUCTION

I find myself faced with a conundrum. It is the possession of a hypothesis, which I quite literally was given by the universe around me. It is like I unwittingly tapped into a source of knowledge that I was not taught in school; and yet, I sit here with this knowledge not knowing exactly where it came from. Moreover, I continue to find evidence which proves it more correct at every step. Even though this problem sits in my own mind as an obstacle, an obstacle of which I am the only creator, I must knock it down and reap the consequences, which are surely to come from the claims of this controversial theory. I have been blessed with a visionary theory, and I cannot help but share it. It may prove to be slightly premature from the standpoint of a traditional perspective; however, even the simplest of theories must begin with a hypothesis. This is all I wish to share – a hypothesis. Maybe there is enough evidence to begin a theory within this text, but for now it will be presented as a hypothesis for those who wish to read, pursue and experiment. Although I share all I have come to know to the point of publication, it is important to state that I did consult experts and cite professionals' works for various pieces of evidence to ensure accuracy. it will be up to the reader to either accept or disprove these concepts in the end. The only potential professional or academic block which may keep this theory from moving forward will be money and politics. This is, of course, unless I have the opportunity to prove it first.

Some ideas may never be scientifically proven and some will just be "known" as truth once they are read by those who are intuitively connected with themselves and the universe around them; but nonetheless, pieces of these theories are available for all to see right in the open in the enigmatic site we call the Giza Plateau. Please seek out this amazing spot. Go there and feel the energy and experience the awe which will stand tall before you;because once you are in its presence, the wonder will never leave you as long as you may live.

It is now safe to say that the theory of the Great Pyramid of Giza, which also goes by other more fitting names, being a tomb is completely unfounded. I say this with confidence, as there has been more evidence gathered proving this theory incorrect than there has been gathered to support it. It has become almost laughable to try and defend the tomb theory as of late. So for the purposes of saving space, time and respecting the curious mind's intelligence and presence of common sense, I will not attempt to prove or disprove the tomb theory in this text. It is time to move on from this archaic philosophy and attempt to grasp the truth. The understood truth shows that this great structure was not a tomb, but a *device* of significance and great importance. This truth is what I will focus on from here forward.

Also, much time and attention has been focused on how the Great Pyramid and other pyramids were built. To get into this debate in this text would be but a distraction, since the reader will find the method of construction is a convoluted and chaotic web of unproven theory, which none have been able to prove nor duplicate. If the method of construction is hard or impossible to duplicate, then it is time to cut our losses and move on to more interesting topics, which still haunt the pyramid mystery. Maybe someone can finally solve the construction mystery after reading this book about what it was used for and explain why it was built.

This really is what the structure is – a mystery within another. It is like a Russian doll but never gives up the final doll or all of its truth. It keeps opening more mysteries. That is, unless one starts in the right place. If one starts looking in the right place and has a bird's eye view of global history and current events, then eventually we can collectively understand some of the mysteries contained within the Great Pyramid to some end. All serious researchers of this wonderful puzzle come into the field from a different perspectives; and so, it is easy to see that each person can bring a piece that can then be built upon by the next researcher. This is what I attempt. I wish to bring another piece of the puzzle by taking into consideration many of the previous researchers, which all have pertinent data and evidence. (mind you, I do not discount or ignore the previous research and/or evidence). All I try to do is take evidence that has already been presented, omit any conclusions, and keep moving forward looking for more evidence, and share my own theory with you. What you find within this text is the latest set of data, which will continue to be built on as the mystery unfolds. I now believe it is time to share my hypothesis with you, as to keep piling up evidence in order to have the perfect conclusion is ultimately unfair to the curious, seekers of truth. It is my opinion that it is better for a large portion of humanity to have a little bit of the truth than it is for a small number to have nearly all the truth. The former is more empowering for humanity than the latter. That being said, I hope you can appreciate an unfinished piece of the puzzle now rather than that of a completed masterpiece many years from now. I think that coming forward with this information now, it may be easier for you to take this to the next step and help humanity know more about the Great Pyramid - and thus, ourselves.

We will know more about ourselves because regardless of which camp you are in, when discussing the origin of the Great Pyramid, once you understand what it is and how it was used, you will find an open door leading to many more questions than answers. Some people think the pyramids were built by primitive ancient Egyptians who hauled chiseled blocks around on logs and dragged them up dirt ramps to drop them in place. Others believe that extraterrestrials came to Earth and either taught primitive humans to build it or that the ETs actually created this pyramid themselves. Another camp thinks that humans were more advanced and knowledgeable than we are today; and thus, they not only had the intelligence to build it, but also technology far greater than we possess today. But no matter which of these "belief camps" you are in, one unifying truth appears that will bring us all together once the reality of the construction and purpose is revealed – and this is a greater understanding of who we are and where we came from. We will learn who we used to be and maybe even where we came from. We will begin to understand why we collectively make decisions in the manner that we do. Much of what we learn about our past could very well show us where we are going. And these considerations are what drive me to present this data and hypothesis to you.

# PART ONE:

## THE SCIENTIFIC THEORY FOR THE USE OF THE GREAT PYRAMID

## 1 MY FIRST ENCOUNTER WITH THE GREAT PYRAMID

So where did this story begin for me, such an unassuming researcher within a saturated field? While I have no traditional honors in Egyptology, anthropology or similar relevant fields to this subject, I do have a Bachelor of Science in Business and have had significant experience in Finance Management and operating small businesses. I am a born trouble shooter. I have grown to question "all-things-life" up to this point. But I must admit there is one main question I never could solve, which every few months of my life would come back to haunt me. That is this enigma: How were the Giza pyramids built and what were their purposes? This came to me from an amazing teacher who did not tow the party line when it came to education. My sixth grade history teacher at the American School In Japan, Mr. Gibson, was not afraid to shine light on the idea that the pyramids were an unanswered riddle. He did walk us through the required text book theory of using ramps, pulleys and logs to drag all the stones in place. But he always chuckled and looked at each and every one of us in the class and asked, "Do any of you really think this is the way the pyramids were built?" Unfailingly, there was a collective "NO" shouted at the top of our lungs. I was especially emotional and emphatic in this response because I always felt that I knew more or that we were being sheltered from the truth. You know our educational system is in a sad state of affairs when a group of sixth graders, even in 1991, knew, collectively, that what they were being fed from the system was garbage. In my opinion, we are not any closer to a reliable pyramid theory today that we were in the education system of 1991.

This paradoxical thought of the pyramid construction quickly burned into my brain. Later that year my parents were planning a trip to go around the world. In short, I moved from the East Coast of the United States when I was ten years old to travel with my family to Japan; and from there, we were given a multitude of opportunities to visit amazing places around the world. I have countless fond memories of growing up and travelling to exotic places, eating wonderful food and learning about cultures, which I would have never learned by sitting and reading about them in school. I also believe it was an important point in my life to be exposed to these wonders because I now recognize that it would not be easy to do the same traveling and exploring in today's post 9/11 culture. Realistically, today's political climate is just difficult to gauge. Additionally, the economy has disabled my ability, and many others' abilities, to spend money on such magnificent explorations. This may or may not be argued to be by design in this era of truth exposure, but I will leave that to another time so as to not get off track.

As this 1991 school year wound to on end my parents asked, "Where shall we go? What does everybody want to see?" I did not hesitate to say I wanted to go to Egypt to see the pyramids. This was always in the forefront of my mind, so I did not let this opportunity to be heard simply slip by me. Come to find out, the rest of the family was also interested in viewing the Great Pyramids, so off we went - Egypt it was! So that is where it began…me as a sixth grader, headed to Egypt for my first (and last up to this date) exploratory trip to Egypt. It does seem sad now that I look back on it. I always thought I would take multiple trips to Egypt to discover and research whatever I wanted. So looking back on it, although I don't regret anything, I do wish I would have taken that trip much more seriously as it manifested. I do not remember the minute details about the trip since I am now closer to 40 than I am 11, but I do remember the primary gut feeling I had as I approached the pyramid, "This thing is a machine. There are precarious things going on in this structure. I cannot go into this building." And so this thought, did in the end, keep me away from engaging in the exploration of the event. So if I could do anything differently, I would have conjured up whatever mojo an eleven year old could possibly have summoned and just did it. I think I could have been writing this book ten years ago instead of today if I had conquered that specific fear. However, everything has its place and time, and it is no accident that I am writing this today. So I will take it at face value and move on!

# 2 CONTRIBUTING THEORIES REGARDING THE PURPOSE OF THE GREAT PYRAMID

There are two major theories that I can share with confidence, which both have compelling evidence showing significant ancient chemical reactions and mechanical workings within the Great Pyramid. The closest theory, which matches the chemical makeup of the reaction I wish to propose, was developed by Christopher Dunn in his book, *The Giza Power Plant: Technologies of Ancient Egypt*. In his book, Dunn identifies how the use of hydrochloric acid and some corresponding chemicals were used to create hydrogen fuel, which the Egyptians or another civilization consumed at the time that it was operational . Another theory I considered was that of John Cadman, with a theory he named "The Great Pyramid's Subterranean Chamber Hydraulic Pulse Generator and Water Pump". In Cadman's theory, he states that the Great Pyramid was designed as a water pump which had the ability to automatically force water vertically. His theory states the need for vertical pumping was to float blocks higher up the construction site . In both of these amazing theories, they rely on the need for each other. However, what is missing from both is critical evidence, which is always assumed to be behind the next block or unexcavated passageway. This is not absent from my theory either, but I do attempt to tie both theories together in a way that identifies a usefulness and a necessity for both ideas.

Dunn's theory is most compelling because it considers two large aspects of the pyramid, which would be integral to the use of the pyramid once it was complete, while Cadman focuses on the pit and the passageways directly connected to it. Dunn focuses his discoveries and evidence on the Queen's Chamber and the King's Chamber, while Cadman puts his effort into the Pit Chamber. So, both theories are relevant and not mutually exclusive, so identifying their theories their entireties and then inspecting their evidence, which they have found on their own as well as compiled from other researchers, will be important to proving any theory regarding the Great Pyramid.

Again, Dunn postulates that the Great Pyramid was a power plant that produced electricity through a chemical reaction with hydrogen. Part of this reaction occurs in the Queen's Chamber through the creation of hydrogen. The other portion of the reaction occurs in the King's Chamber. Dunn's evidence of these reactions will be identified later. However, what seems to be lacking in Dunn's theory is focus on the purpose of the Pit Chamber. This is most likely because he had not quite found enough evidence to bring forth its true purpose. This is understandable because it is not easy to bring the past into the present when so much previous exploration might have vacated some necessary evidence to help Dunn in his pursuit. That being said, where Dunn left off, John Cadman picks up.

John Cadman developed a theory that examined the shape of the Pit area, starting at the descending passage and going all the way to the pit well, including the unexplored shaft protruding horizontally. He also postulates that the pump had enough power to force liquid to the top of the pyramid. Although he awakens the notion that the entire pyramid was used as a water pump for the whole Giza plateau, he does not revere the evidence Dunn set forth, which is compelling and hard to ignore. It is possible to see with Cadman's pump theory that water or some other liquid could be sent up the pyramid to flow out of the top and irrigate the Giza plateau. However, that is just one piece of the puzzle and does not explain the purpose of the King and Queen's Chambers. Furthermore it does not explain some of the chemical residue evidence, which will be discussed later.

Although both of these theories make much sense, as we will see later, it is important to highlight what the two theories and evidence from both of these theories demonstrate. They are not indicating that the pyramid is just a water pump or just an electric or hydrogen power plant. They are revealing that we must consider the evidence from both; and thus, we must either consider an additional use or contemplate a completely different theory all together.

That said, I do not endeavor to prove they are both wrong in my hypothesis. I am only attempting to illustrate how my new discoveries might compliment these two theories and may bring them all together as "one set" of evidence. A new purpose is glaring as to what the pyramid was used for in ancient times. However, with more answers, we develop more questions, and all I can do is take the baton from the work that already exists and prepare it for the next puzzle assembler. So much exciting work is yet to be done with regards to the enigma we face, which is called The

Great Pyramid of Giza. I look forward to seeing what can be unearthed next.

While this is possibly not the end explanation for the pyramids, it will at least inspire the next baton carrier to take humanity to the next level in understanding itself, and thus, the pyramid. Because that is exactly what the pyramid is – a representation of our knowledge of the past, present and the future. The more we learn about ourselves and what we are capable of, the more we understand about this mystery we call the Great Pyramid. I am convinced that the more we focus on how it was made and what its purpose was, the more we learn about who we are, where we came from and where we will be.

So regardless of what you believe to be true about the theory I am about to present, do me and humanity one last favor, as if this were my death bed confession - go forth and learn about yourself. Do not be afraid of the truth, even as it stares at you and challenges you. Be open-minded and carry yourself as an empty vessel. Fill your vessel with whatever knowledge you can - every day. Then contemplate that knowledge as you fall asleep, and wake up the next day with yet another empty vessel again. Now, I cannot guarantee you will find all the answers you seek by following this advice, but I can assure you that will have room for the truth as it comes to you. With an empty vessel, you will be humble and know the truth when it arrives.

# 3 EVIDENCE FROM CONTRIBUTING THEORIES

Christopher Dunn identifies a major chemical reaction which was taking place in the Queen's Chamber. Dunn claims that a chemical reaction using hydrochloric acid and a zinc catalyst solution was used to create hydrogen, and the hydrogen was harvested to power the Giza plateau. His theory states that the hydrogen was created and then sound was used in the King's chamber to resonate with the gas and charge it in a way that could make it useful and transportable via microwave beam or LASER/MASER technology. This very well could be the case, but I do not think it answers all of the questions as to how the entire structure could have been used. Although his evidence is compelling, it is not simple enough to allow an automated series of stages. I think it is important to identify the simplest reaction *first* so that we can then move on to the more complicated functions. So for the purposes of simplicity and respect of Dunn's work, I will not disagree with his theory of the Great Pyramid being a Power Plant. In fact I do think he is right. I do not have enough evidence to disprove or prove his theory on way or another, but I think he does a wonderful job of describing the "Power Plant" theory in his work.

The focus of this work, however, is the idea that my theory could be considered the "prequel" to Dunn's work. In other words, I will introduce the simplest reaction that can occur within the structure of the pyramid. Please note, some of this evidence has not been discovered, but it does not disprove what you are about to read. Much of the pyramid is still being revealed and discovered, and the shafts are largely unexplored. So even though a little imagination is required to complete the cycle of the reaction, it is quite easy to see what was transpiring there, once a nudge is given to the reader.

As stated previously, much of Dunn's work does revolve around the idea of storing or housing Hydrochloric Acid in the Queen's Chamber, so that is where we will start in this process. In my theory, Hydrochloric Acid was not being created in this chamber, but it was being stored there for future use elsewhere within the structure. Here is Dunn's description of the Queen's Chamber activities:

> There are two shafts leading to this chamber which were bored into the wall block and terminated five inches from the inside wall of the chamber, leaving what Smyth described as a "left". The discovery of these enigmatic shafts came in 1872 when Waynman Dixon was able to thrust a rod through a small crack in an otherwise perfectly fitted wall and then chiseled through the limestone. Dixon noted that the limestone "left" was particularly soft in that area. Emboldened by this important discovery he measured off the same distance on the other wall and discovered another shaft. [1]
>
> [Piazzi] Smyth [a pyramid researcher from the late 1800's] is credited for noting another anomaly in the Queen's Chamber—there were flakes of white mortar exuding from stone joints inside the shaft. Analysis of the mortar found it to be plaster of paris—gypsum (calcium sulfate). Smyth also described this chamber as having a foul odor, which caused early visitors to the chamber to beat a hasty retreat, and it was assumed that tourists were relieving themselves, though the way Smyth described this chamber, few people stayed long enough to do so. [2]
>
> One of the greatest mysteries of this chamber has been the salt encrustation on the walls. It was up to one-half-inch thick in places, and Petrie took it into account when he made measurements of the chamber. The salt also was found along the Horizontal Passage and in the lower portion of the Grand Gallery. [3]
>
> The flood and groundwater theories do not account for the salt found in the Great Pyramid, but proponents of these theories might be right about one thing—the existence of the salt itself suggests that the Queen's Chamber was designed to take in fluid rather than air. The power plant theory explains why fluid may have been introduced into the pyramid and how it produced the salt encrustations on the walls. Nearly all of the facts that have so mystified Egyptologists fit logically together if the Queen's Chamber was once used to create hydrogen to fuel this power plant. Salt is a natural by-product of the reaction designed to produce hydrogen. It would form

when the hot, hydrogen-bearing gas reacted with the calcium in the pyramid's limestone walls. If the half-inch of salt on the Queen's Chamber walls were the result of repeated inundations—not of water—of chemicals, those used to create the fuel that powered the plant, it is unlikely that any of this chemical fluid would find its way into the bottom part of the Grand Gallery. The orientation of the passage leading from the Queen's Chamber would take the chemicals down into the Well Shaft and into the Subterranean Pit. Because the greatest concentration of heat would be inside the Queen's Chamber, with a gradual cooling off as the gas made its way into the Grand Gallery, the buildup of salt would diminish along with the heat. This process would account for the presence of salt in the Queen's Chamber and other parts of the pyramid and also for its uneven distribution in these areas. The kind of salt that is created in a chemical process depends on the chemicals involved in generating the gas. I am not going to argue for a particular combination of chemicals, and say that is the combination the ancient Egyptians used. But I will present one feasible combination—suggested to me by a chemical engineer—with the understanding that the pyramid builders may have used a different one. [4]

Importantly, please note Dunn admits here that there could be more than one reason or reaction to create salt.

Gypsum also is produced through the action of sulfuric acid on limestone, and, although this in itself does not prove that sulfur and/or its by-products were used in the chemical process in this chamber, it does promote the consideration of other data in a new light. Because the pyramid's building materials contain one of the elements needed to produce gypsum (the limestone masonry), it follows that the introduction either accidental or purposeful—of another necessary element (sulfuric acid, for instance) would produce gypsum. Several questions come to mind in light of the preceding speculations. They may be totally unrelated, but it would be interesting to know the answers to the following: Was the disgusting smell that caused early explorers to beat a hasty retreat from the chamber connected to a chemical process that used sulfur? Hydrogen sulfide is particularly odorous, exuding a smell similar to rotten eggs. This gas is formed by the combination of sulfur with hydrogen. While early explorers expected to be confronted with a certain amount of bat dung inside the pyramid, it seemed as though the smell in this particular chamber was more pronounced than in the rest of the pyramid. Again, the composition of the salts on the chamber's walls may help clarify this investigation, as sulfur-bearing compounds may have formed these salts. Where did Caviglia get the chunks of sulfur that he burned in the Well Shaft? While it was a practice of early explorers to burn sulfur to purify unhealthy air, it would be most helpful to know whether or not he had the sulfur with him or if it was already there. If a chemical exchange process was separating hydrogen and if a catalyst was being used in the Queen's Chamber, would sulfur plays part in the operation or perhaps regeneration of the catalyst?1 The shafts leading to the Queen's Chamber revealed other oddities that may help our investigation into its true function. In these channels, explorers found a small bronze grapnel hook, a piece of wood, and a stone ball. [5]

Several questions remain unanswered regarding the discovery of these items, and the items themselves, that prevent any assertion as to their intended purpose: Was there just one of each item? Were they found together in the same shaft? Were they in any way connected? Was their removal from the shaft difficult or easy? [6]

...all these seemingly unexplained facts fall into place, if our explanation is founded on the basic premise that some kind of chemical reaction was taking place there.

I was hoping to be able to get into the Queen's Chamber while I was in Egypt in 1986 to get a sample of the salt for analysis. I had speculated that the salt on the walls of the chamber was an unwanted, though significant, residual substance caused by a chemical reaction where hot hydrogen reacted with the limestone. Unfortunately, I was unable to get into the chamber because a French team was already inside the Horizontal Passage, boring holes into what they hoped were additional chambers. (It was discovered, after I left Egypt, that the spaces contained only sand.)...

...In 1978, Dr. Patrick Flanagan asked the Arizona Bureau of Geology and Mineral Technology to analyze a sample of this salt. They found it to be a mixture of calcium carbonate (limestone), sodium chloride (halite or salt), and calcium sulfate (gypsum, also known as plaster of paris). These are precisely the minerals that would be produced by the reaction of hot, hydrogen-bearing gas with the limestone walls and ceiling of the Queen's Chamber. Armed with this information, I sought out a chemical engineer, Joseph Drejewski, to see if my perception regarding the Queen's Chamber was plausible. He was skeptical about my entire premise but agreed to look at the data and form an evaluation. I had speculated that the five-inch "left"—which contained a small hole through to the channel—that prevented each shaft from joining with the Queen's Chamber was intentionally designed to meter a specific amount of fluid into the chamber over a period of time. If we knew the head pressure of the fluid, we could accurately calculate the amount of fluid that flowed through this "left". One of these two shafts has a different discoloration, or staining, and I speculated that this was the result of the ancient Egyptians introducing two different chemicals into the chamber, which, when combined, would produce a reaction. Drejewski agreed that two chemical solutions could be introduced into this chamber to create hydrogen or ammonia under ambient conditions of 80° Fahrenheit, ± 20°. He agreed that the niche in the wall of the chamber could have been used to house a cooling or evaporation tower. The corbelled niche inside the reaction chamber would have provided an anchor for this tower, which also may have contained a catalyst. One scenario could be that the chemicals pooled on the floor of the chamber and wicked through the catalyst material. The offset of the niche may indicate the proportion of each chemical introduced into the chamber. Drejewski, therefore, agreed that my theory was plausible. To evaluate my theory further, we must now move from considering the technology of this machine to the fuel that ran it. Let us consider how hydrogen is made and used to produce energy. Drejewski prepared a report informing me of the following: Hydrogen is most easily obtained by displacing it from acids by contact with certain metals that are more active than hydrogen and therefore will combine more readily with the other constituents of the acid. Zinc (Zn) is the most commonly chosen metal and when treated with dilute hydrochloric acid (HCl), it will produce a reasonably pure hydrogen gas which evolves at a relatively fast rate. The hydrogen gas produced by this reaction of zinc with hydrochloric acid may contain water vapor carried along by the gas as it bubbles through the water solution. If impurities are present, it is possible to remove the water vapor (with the impurity) bypassing the generated gas over or through a drying agent such as calcium chloride (Ca Cl2), which retains the water vapor, but does not react with the hydrogen gas. Other metals which can be used [as a drying agent] are magnesium and finely divided iron (powder). [7]

Drejewski ended his evaluation by cautiously stating, "It is highly probable that [through this reaction] impurities such as calcium sulfate (gypsum) and sodium chloride (halite) can be leached through limestone [calcium carbonate] (Ca CO3 )." I have been asked by other researchers who have reviewed a synopsis of my theory whether electrolysis could have played a part in the generation of hydrogen. I am not going to rule that out completely, but electrolysis would require only one shaft leading to the chamber, as it is a process using only water and electrical power. We have to explain the reasons for two similar shafts, and the dark staining inside the Northern Shaft. This staining clearly indicates the use of two different chemicals. Additional evidence to support the theory that chemicals were flowing down these shafts came in 1993, when Rudolph Gantenbrink guided his robot Upuaut II up the Southern Shaft and discovered the so-called "door" with its copper fittings. We will remember that Smyth noted gypsum exuding from the joints of the Southern Shaft leading to the Queen's Chamber. The filming of this channel by Gantenbrink's robot revealed signs of erosion in the lower portion of the shaft. The walls and floor of the channel were extremely rough, and the erosion of the walls appeared to have horizontal striations. There also were signs of what appeared to be gypsum leaching from the limestone walls.

Gantenbrink's robot came to a dead end at the upper part of the Southern Shaft. It encountered a block of limestone with two mysterious copper fittings protruding through it. It was widely publicized that a hidden door had been found inside the Great Pyramid. What was not publicized, however, is that the shaft itself is only about nine inches square.

While I was watching the video of the exploration with my friend, Jeff Summers, he off-handedly remarked that the fittings looked like electrodes. His observation made sense to me. To deliver an accurate measure of hydrochloric acid solution to the reaction chamber, a certain head pressure would need to be maintained. The head pressure is determined by the volume of fluid in the channel, that is, the weight of the column of chemical. The copper fittings would have served as a switch to signal the need for more chemicals. Floating on the surface of the fluid would have been another part of this switch—the cedarlike wood joined together with the bronze grapnel hook. This assembly would rise and fall with the fluid in the channel. With the channel full, the bronze prongs would have made contact with the electrodes, creating a circuit, and as the fluid in the channel dropped, the prongs would move away from the electrodes, thereby breaking the contact and acting as a switch to signal the pumping of more chemical solution into the channel until the bronze hook again made contact with the electrodes. As the rate of supply into the reaction chamber was slight, a small opening was all that was needed to maintain the supply of chemicals. [8]

On the other hand, the texture of the walls and floor of the shaft at the lower level—as photographed by Gantenbrink—was deeply eroded, with horizontal striations, and there also appeared to be leaching of salts on the surface of the ceiling and the walls. Both of these conditions could have been caused by a chemical fluid. But Danley detected something else. The device heard a secondary echo. This echo was produced by the sound squeezing through the small gap at the bottom of the door and traveling through into the space beyond, the space where Gantenbrink had offered to go with another robot but was denied the opportunity. Danley's instrument told him that the sound wave traveled another thirty feet before bouncing back to the source.

A hint of what might be there came in 1992 when French engineer and professor Jean Leherou Kerisel, and his team, conducted ground-penetrating radar and microgravimetry tests in the short horizontal passage that leads from the Descending Passage to the Subterranean Pit. He detected a structure under the floor of the passageway which he analyzed as possibly being a corridor oriented SSE-NNW and with a ceiling at the same depth that the Descending Passage would have reached had it been continued.

A second very clear anomaly, a "mass defect" as Kerisel calls it, "was detected on the western side of the passageway six metres before the chamber entrance. According to our calculations, this anomaly corresponds to a vertical shaft at least five metres deep with a section of about 1.40 Å— 1.40 metres very close to the western wall of the passageway." In short, what Kerisel believes he has identified off the Subterranean Chamber's entrance corridor is something that looks very much like a completely separate passageway system, terminating in a vertical shaft. His instruments may have misled him, or, as he himself admits, he may merely have picked up the traces of "a large volume of limestone dissolved by the action of underground water—in other words a deep cave". Alternatively, however, if the "mass defect" turns out to be a man-made feature, as he strongly suspects, then "it may lead to very interesting developments."5 Kerisel's findings indicate that the supply shafts leading to the Queen's Chamber may have been supplied with chemicals by means of a vertical shaft that connected to an underground chamber. It should be noted that Kerisel detected the vertical anomaly on the west side of the passageway. The shafts leading to the Queen's Chamber are oriented to the west of the passageway. In light of my proposed use for these shafts, and of Kerisel's discovery, it would not be out of order for us to postulate that when Gantenbrink's "door" is penetrated, or when the clandestine diggers above the King's Chamber reach their destination, a vertical shaft leading to a bedrock chamber will be found. I also would not be surprised if more copper, in the form of cables or wires that had been attached to the "copper fittings," are found beyond Gantenbrink's "door". We can now understand how chemicals were introduced to the Queen's Chamber and caused a reaction that filled all the cavities within the Great Pyramid. [9]

At the juncture where the Horizontal Passage meets the Ascending Passage is a five-inch lip. There may have been a slab resting against this lip and bridged between the Ascending Passage and the floor of the Grand Gallery, where a similar lip is found. Slots in the sidewall indicate that there may have been supporting members for this slab, which would have had holes drilled into it to allow the gas to rise into the Grand Gallery. Spent chemical solution from the Queen's Chamber would have flowed along the Horizontal Passage and down the Well Shaft into either the Grotto or, if the shaft at that time connected to the lower Descending Passage, the Subterranean Pit below. The lip and a bridging slab would have prevented the fluid from flowing down the Ascending Passage. [10]

shafts leading to the Queen's Chamber but not quite connected to it. These could have been supply shafts for chemicals needed in the reaction. The shafts would allow chemicals to enter the chamber and prevent evolving gases from escaping. Flakes of gypsum [were] exuding from joints in shafts. This substance probably resulted from the chemical reacting with limestone (suggesting the use of sulfuric acid). buildup of salt crystals on the walls and ceiling of the Queen's Chamber, Horizontal Passage, and lower level of Grand Gallery. This buildup was likely the result of gaseous vapor passing over the limestone, reacting with the calcium in the limestone, and giving up water and impurities. This was a by-product from the drying of the gas. [11]

When Howard-Vyse's men blasted through tons of limestone and granite and discovered the four chambers above Davison's Chamber, the first part they went into had a strange effect on them. They crawled out of the air space covered from head to toe with a fine, thin black powder. The floor of the chamber was covered with it. Analysis of the powder showed it to be exuviae, the cast-off shells and skins of insects. Insect shells are comprised mainly of calcium carbonate, and if we look for a source for calcium carbonate in the area, we find it in the core limestone masonry itself. As the crushed limestone hung in the air it quite literally could have cooked in the elevated temperatures of the [theoretical] hydrogen explosion and the fire that followed. The black calcium carbonate dust would have settled finally onto the tops of the granite beams.

Perhaps the coffer was originally red, quarried at the same time, in the same place, as the rest of the granite used to construct the King's Chamber. It is possible, therefore, that the granite box, because of its thinner construction, did not have the ability to conduct the heat to which it was subjected and so it simply overcooked, causing the color change. Architect Jim Hagan, who is an expert in the application of stonework in construction, explained to me that the interior chambers of the Great Pyramid have the appearance of being subjected to extreme temperatures; and he claimed that the broken corner on the granite box shows signs of being melted, rather than simply being chipped away. [12]

So with all of this evidence pointing towards a hydrochloric acid containment in the Queen's Chamber, then we need to identify how and where they were able to make this hydrochloric acid. This reactive acid is quite dangerous to transport, so I suspect the Ancient Egyptians did not make it too far away from the pyramid. What if there was some evidence showing that the pyramid itself could be a laboratory where this reactive chemical was manufactured? To me, this would make a lot more sense than trying to speculate where and how the civilization was able to produce it offsite and then safely transport it onsite. There is quite a bit of circumstantial evidence that points toward it actually being produced inside the pyramid. Later on I will discuss this revelation when we further examine the flow of the machine. However, to share a small hint now, before we see the machine in action, suffice it to say that hydrochloric acid would not be the first chemical produced within the pyramid. I believe it would actually be the third. Again, this will be explained in greater detail later in the book. Nonetheless, this process must be shown in different stages, and we will see from the creation of the first few chemicals inside the structure how hydrochloric acid can be made. All three major chambers are necessary for its production.

The well shaft was identified by Dunn to be a construction, which was undertaken after the pyramid was completed. Furthermore, it was actually made after it had been running for quite some time and some repair was needed to get it running again: "It evidently shows that the passage mouth was cut out after the building was finished in that part. It is clear, then, that the whole of this shaft is an additional feature to the first plan." [13]

It is also important to note that evidence of another essential component to my chemical reaction theory was found by a Colonel Vyse in 1836 and then tested by Dr Jones and Dr. El Gayer in 1989. Vyse discovered a flat chunk of Iron and catalogued it. This piece of evidence was then revisited by Jones and El Gayer and optically tested for elemental make up; it was found to be made of iron and contained gold deposits on it. It is important to note, for further discussion, that in the reaction flow this item was discovered in the King's Chamber:

In 1989 it was subjected to scientific analysis. The tests were done by Dr. Jones in the mineral resources engineering department at Imperial College and Dr. El Gayer in the department of petroleum and mining at the Suez University. They utilized both chemical and optical tests. One hypothesis was that the metal may have come from a meteorite. It have been well documented that primitive and stone age peoples have used meteorite iron for implements, etc. They were able to make crude iron implements from the meteorite iron well before the iron age. In fact, wrapped in King Tut's mummy was a dagger made of meteorite iron. How do we know if the iron is from a meteorite or made by man? We can determine this from the iron's nickel content. Meteorite iron has a higher value than the iron found on earth. The analysis of the metal plate yielded the following: "the iron plate from Giza is clearly not of meteoritic origin, since it contains only a trace of nickel". Further analysis revealed that it had traces of gold on its surface, maybe once gold plated. Drs. Jones and Gayer concluded the following:

It is concluded, on the basis of the present investigation, that the iron plate is very ancient. Furthermore, the metallurgical evidence supports the archeological evidence which suggests that the plate was incorporated within the pyramid at the time that structure was being built. [14]

A possible explanation for discovery of this piece of metal with traces of gold left on its surface, which will make sense in the reaction flow charts later, is that it was originally lining the shafts in the King's Chamber, or at least in part of the shafts. This would be necessary to create an electrical circuit. In his book, *Before the Pharohs*, Edward F. Malkowski hints at the idea of the shafts being gold plated, "…[The shaft] was constructed to pass through the masonry from the north face of the pyramid into the king's chamber… Lining the shafts with gold plated iron would make it a very efficient conduit for the input signal and power output." (*Before the Pharaohs: Egypt's Mysterious Prehistory* (p.128) By Edward F. Malkowski).

Therefore when looking at Dunn, Dr. Jones, Dr. El Gayer and Malkowski's works, it becomes ostensible that there must have been some type of chemical reaction taking place in the Great Pyramid. However, without working parts and movement it seems quite far-fetched that anything could really be happening inside the structure without external intervention or humans shoveling material or transporting this chemicals manually around the pyramid. To most, it would not make sense because at least one of the chemicals identified by Dunn (others and myself), it would not have been safe. In fact, using those chemicals in such large quantities would have been nothing short of deadly. Moreover, to be in the same room with those chemicals, even with the most sophisticated safety gear we have today, (including hazmat suits and nuclear protection gear) would categorically be insufficient and short lived in the face of such highly concentrated acids. So with this in mind, I must conclude that it was automated to some degree, if not completely automated.

The first question one would ask after bringing up "automation" would most likely be, "Where did they get the power? There wasn't any electricity when the pyramids were finished for thousands of years, let alone when they were being built." However, I have just two words to refute this argument: "Baghdad Battery." It was recently proven that these amazing devices (discovered in Iraq), which came from the Sumerian era civilization, were designed to carry a stored electric charge not unlike the batteries we use today. Yes, the Iraqi's, or Sumerians to be precise, did develop this technology long before western civilization did. I will just refer you to Smith College's research into this apparatus. Refer to the work of Dennielle Downs and Ava Meyerhoff, discussed below: [15]

The Baghdad Battery is just one example of how electricity could be used to activate switches and turn apparatuses on and off within the structure. For argument's sake we will assume his device could be replicated and placed in a series or parallel to create whatever voltage or amperage needed to satisfy electrical needs. I do think it is appropriate to assume the entire civilization ran on these batteries, but it is safe to say that potentially some devices were initially activated by them. Not unlike your own vehicle; you do not run your entire vehicle for months on end with a battery alone (with the exception of new electric car technology) but you would start your engine with this battery. That is all we would need to assume to make this technology work at this stage.

Next issue to identify and resolve would be the idea that electric switches and valves by themselves will not alone move anything substantial. An inordinate amount of battery power would be needed to move large amounts of massive substances. So there must be some sort of built in mechanism designed to move the liquids throughout the complex. All of Dunn's evidence, while compelling and novel, does not address one glaring issue. The first question I would ask once seeing all of this circumstantial evidence pointing towards some sort of chemical reaction within the pyramid is this, "What could possibly run this giant beaker and transfer all of the chemicals from one chamber to the next?" That is a concept I battled with for a while before stumbling onto the next piece of this mysterious puzzle. The person who has identified the most conspicuous potentiality is a man named John Cadman. A pump would suffice but is there a pump or even remnants of a pump anywhere in the pyramid? Yes there is. Cadman has identified it and reverse engineered one. Although it utilizes a large portion of the entire pyramid structure to work the main components necessary to function sit under the ground surface and in the Pit.

Cadman postulated that there is a giant autonomous pump mechanism built right into the pyramid just as deliberately planned as any of the other more known features. This pump would have been able to house a beaker like chamber, agitate solutions and run fluid throughout the shaft systems and thus the chambers and the whole structure.

Cadman names his pump "The Great Pyramid's Subterranean Chamber Hydraulic Pulse Generator and Water Pump" and it is most aptly identified. Cadman proclaims, "The whole pyramid can be removed and the pump mechanism will still be present. It is a very simple yet effective device. If I'm right about the ancients having built this device then they were geniuses. If I'm wrong about them building the device then I'm certainly willing to take credit for this marvelous machine." So according to his workup the pump may have been not only the first device designed in the blueprints, it looks to be the most important. Below we'll take a look at his findings.

Cadman identifies the proper device as the "Hydraulic Ramp Pump." [16] Noted below are his findings:

> Before any theorizing about the Great Pyramid, a little pump background is helpful. Invented in the 1700's, hydraulic ram pumps are a primitive but highly effective machine. These simple pumps incorporate only two moving parts. Used extensively around the world until the invention of the electric water pump, these pumps have nearly been forgotten. The basic design utilizes the force of falling water to elevate part of the water (see Figure 3). Water flows down the drive pipe into the compression chamber. Water escapes from the waste valve until the water's velocity forces the valve shut. When the valve shuts, the water stops flowing instantaneously and causes the water to compress resulting in a compression wave, or shock wave, to emanate from the valve area. In the drive line, the water reverses direction until the shock wave reaches air and returns down the pipe. In the output line, a

high pressure surge passes through the check valve. This surge is at least fifty times (3,360 psi at Giza) the static water pressure of the compression chamber. When the compression wave leaves the compression chamber, a low pressure situation exists. The low pressure is equal and opposite to the compression wave. This immediately re-opens the waste valve. The stand pipe is a shortcut for the compression wave to reach air. Once the compression wave reaches air, a wave returns down the stand pipe and starts the water flow back into the compression chamber. The stand pipe, usually twice the diameter of the drive pipe, allows for the highest possible cycling rate.

Most hydraulic ram pumps are free standing, with the majority of parts being exposed above ground (see Figure 3). A specialized application is to have the lines underground (see Figure 4). The stand pipe needs to exit to air, and the waste valve (wastegate) also needs an exit. To facilitate the waste valve output, a line may be extended from the compression chamber to an appropriate location. This allows for the bulk of the pump lines to be centrally located. This layout has an interesting side effect - the compression wave becomes focused in the line leading to the compression chamber and this focused compression wave transmits a pulse through the compression chamber's ceiling.

Fig 3

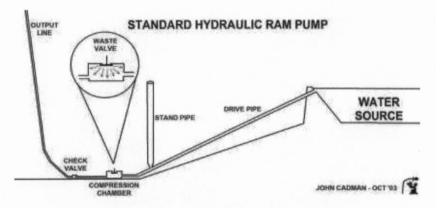

The basic hydraulic ram pump has water running from the elevated water source to the compression chamber. A valve in the compression chamber allows water to flow out until the velocity forces the valve shut. The valve shutting causes a high pressure spike that forces water past the check valve and through the output line. The waste valve reopens and once again allows water to flow down the pipe. The stand pipe affects the cycle rate by creating a shortcut for the reverse surge.

Fig. 4

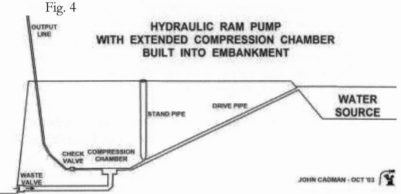

Building an underground ram pump requires lengthening of the compression chamber to allow for waste water output. This is the layout of the functioning machine for this article. It could not be any simpler or more effective. Design: John Cadman Patent pending

Fig.

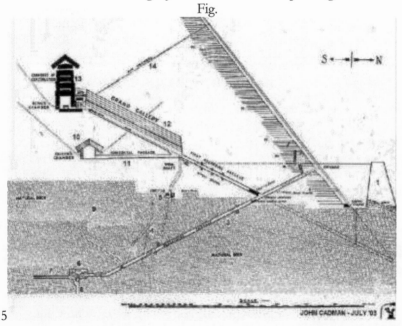

5

Before theorizing about missing parts, it is important to view what is known to have existed. Although the retaining wall (1) no longer is in existence, it is an accepted part of the complex. The retaining walls and casing stones were dismantled for building materials for Cairo.

The subterranean chamber (6) is the largest and most unusual room of the Great Pyramid. This odd looking room is located 100' below the base of the Great Pyramid and carved from the solid limestone bedrock of the plateau (see Figure 5). This large room is 27' north to south and 56' east to west. The entrance is near the floor at the northeast corner. The eastern half of the room averages 11' to 13' in height. The western half of the room is a 5 ½' high step (see Figure 6). The step has a channel in the middle that leads to the western wall. This channel, the "step channel", starts at floor level but tapers as it heads towards the back wall. On top of the step are two fins that run from the front of the step to the back wall. A third fin starts ½ way back on the step. All of the fins run east to west and reach up near the ceiling. On the main floor there is a {6'} wide square pit set diagonally some 5' from the eastern wall. This pit drops 5 ½' to a step where the pit narrows to 4' square. The total depth of the pit is about 11' although Cavigula had drilled down another 30' in the 1800's.5 In the southeastern corner is the entrance to a tunnel that measures 29" by 31". Dubbed the "dead end" shaft, this tunnel runs 57' due south where it ends in a vertical wall.

The subterranean chamber has confounded most pyramid researchers. The Orthodox camp essentially gave up trying to explain this room. They came up with the idea that the whole subterranean section was a giant mistake. Edward Kunkel, Chris Dunn, and Joe Parr gave alternate views. Kunkel was partially correct when he recognized that the chamber was part of a modified hydraulic ram pump. Dunn recognized that the chamber must be the location for the source of a pulse direct towards King's chamber. Parr recognized that it was the location of a sound transmission.

Fig. 6

Spencer L. Cross

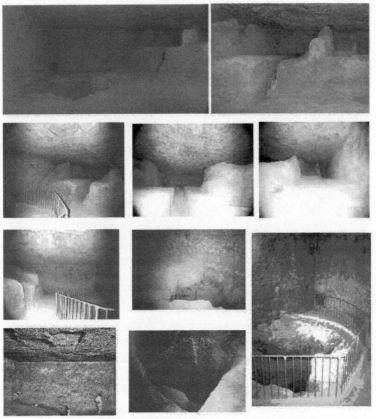

It is difficult to describe the largest room of the Great Pyramid. Upon entering the room we are faced with a pit tunneled in the middle of the floor. One half of the room is a large step with odd fins. The handrail around the pit was added in modern times to prevent visitors from falling into it. Photos: Guardian's Giza, Edgar Brothers, GPG-RA

Fig. 7

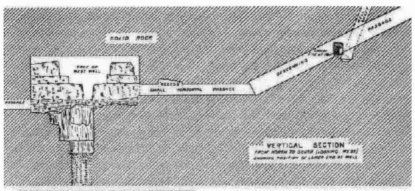

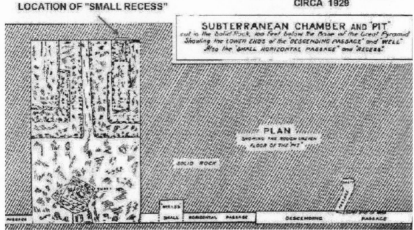

Although these drawings were a primary source for the models, they have errors in the finned area. The fin errors were a result of the fins being filled with rubble when the sketch was done. The bottom drawing shows the location of the small recess that corresponds to the best location for an air or gas removal line. It should be noted that Perring excavated the pit another 36 feet back in the 1800's, but that has since been filled back in.

The pyramid had a tall masonry enclosure that was higher than the pyramid's entrance (1) (see Figure 8). Water was flooded between this masonry wall and the pyramid via tunnels from the ancient Lake Moeris (2). Lake Moeris and the Western Nile were at higher elevations and allowed for water tunnels to gravity feed to this pyramid's moat1,3 (see Figure 2). One of the water tunnels existed as a "well" in front of the pyramid's entrance. This well has since been covered with pavement1. As the moat filled, water flooded the entrance and ran down the descending passage (3) into the subterranean chamber (6).

Fig. 8

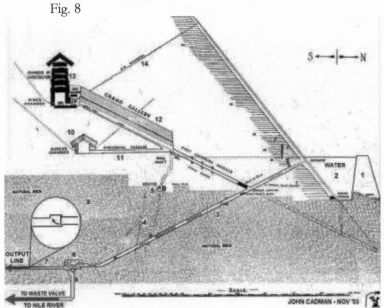

The pump assembly incorporates the descending passage (3), subterranean chamber (6), the "dead end" shaft (7), the pit (8), the well shaft (4) and grotto (5). To complete the basic hydraulic ram, two blocked tunnels need to be cleared. At the end of the "dead end" shaft exists a plane surface that correlates to the back side of a check-valve. The pit hasn't been completely excavated to expose the horizontal shaft. In the running model the water in the well shaft pulsed at the grotto height even though this is below moat elevation.

Fig. 9

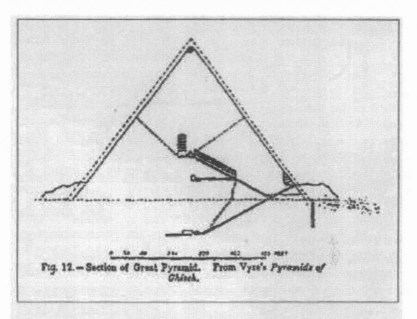

Fig. 12.—Section of Great Pyramid. From Vyse's *Pyramids of Gizeh.*

15. Section of Great Pyramid from Vyse's *Pyramids of Gizeh*, 1839, showing well in front of entrance.

The well in front of the entrance would have been connected to the ancient Lake Moeris which was at a higher elevation than the Great Pyramid. Lake Moeris was the size of lake Erie. Water would have gravity fed from the lake to the walled enclosure.

At the lower end of the descending passage a tunnel leads up towards the lowest of the two upper rooms. This shaft is known as the "well shaft" (4). Until the late 1800's most of the descending passage, the lower part of the well shaft and the subterranean chamber had been buried for a thousand years2. Indigenous teachings state emphatically that there is still a buried tunnel that leads from the bottom of the subterranean chamber's pit (8) (see Figure 8) to the location of the ancient Nile River3. This tunnel was a drain that had a mechanical element at its end. This mechanical element is possibly a sliding stone plug, which opened and closed causing a pulsing action (see Figure 24). The "dead end" shaft (7) terminates 57' past it's entrance. It is my hypothesis that the termination is the back face of a closed check valve, and a tunnel exists beyond (see inset Figure 8).

To maintain consistent pulse timing, the pyramid's moat requires a specific static level. To ensure this, the moat is provided more water than is consumed. The excess water was removed by the causeway running down to the Nile River. [16]

Without taking too much away from Cadman's work it is appropriate to end here with citations of his work. I would highly recommend visiting his website in order to  watch this amazing device in action.  It is quite apparent that this pump is functional once you watch his demonstration. It not only clearly shows the pump running successfully, it also shows it pulsating, which would create a turbulent atmosphere within the chamber. Identifying this "pulsing" is important because one of the steps required in the chemical reaction theory is an agitation in the Pit, so liquid can quickly dissolve certain solid additives.  We will see this in action shortly.

Although Cadman is rightly confident that the Pit complex is an integral piece showing how most of the lower portion of the pyramid was designed to pump water, I am not sure he truly understands how close he was to the true purpose and significance of his findings.  In other words,  if he had put a couple of more pieces of the puzzle together with his findings, I believe he would be the one writing this theory today and not myself.  This is also fair to say with regards to Dunn's work as well.  If they had collaborated, even in just the slightest manner, I think they would have had gone to press with this idea and may have gone further in the popularity of their work. Instead, the combination of the two theories rest here.

# 4 THE HOLISTIC PYRAMID REACTION

We now understand how a chemical reaction might have been taking place in the Great Pyramid. Dunn has identified this; and I agree to a large extent that not only was this taking place, but the chemicals being stored in the Queen's Chamber were correct. In my opinion, where he falls short is bringing the totality of the reaction to a close and possibly overlooking additional reactions or even potentially putting reactions in the correct order. Also lacking is the details about what was stored in the King's Chamber. The King's and Queen's chambers rest above the Pit, and both chambers have gentle sloping passageways, which all eventually lead to the Pit. If everything leads to the Pit and gravity is relevant in any Earthly process, then we must conclude that both chambers were allowing a release of substance to the Pit for some reason.

We also know that based on Cadman's discoveries, and invention, that a pump was active within the pyramid. This pump was undeniably focused in the pit structure and chamber. It had the ability to not only pump fluid linearly; it was also able to pump it vertically. All of this process was free standing and automated once the device was activated by valves and electrical stimulation. So if reactions were taking place and fluid was being moved around the structure for various activities, then where was it going, what was being made, and why? Although we will discuss the "where and what" right now, the "why" will be discussed in part two of this text. For purposes of proving the theory, we will only focus on the reaction, movement and the end product. The "why" it was being made is actually what brought me to this specific set of reactions to begin with, but it is a more subjective, philosophical and theological perspective; hence, that portion of the analysis will be delivered in a separate discussion.

My thoughts on the reaction in the pyramid are driven by attempting to simplify the purpose of the structure as much as I possibly could without disregarding the major principles already discovered by Dunn and Cadman. When it comes to building major structures, there really is not a lot of "fluff" involved (unless you are building a hotel in Dubai), so that is the approach I took when reverse engineering the Pyramid. Art versus function is always the age-old battle between the architect's creation of a majestic structure and the artist's vision of its innovation. Although the designer must try and make the building as aesthetically pleasing as possible, it must hold people, house working utilities and stay upright. Those are today's major goals in designing safe, beautiful buildings. So was the pyramid art? No. At least it was not art as its main purpose. It was not a tomb, which I would also categorize as art. This is mainly discerned the same way many visual decisions are made. How do you know if something is art? The artistic observer must be able to define it as such. There is plenty of art all over Egypt, and there are also plenty of tombs, but never has a pyramid been scientifically proven or identified as to house a body at any time. The pyramid was a functional structure with great purpose. What was this majestic purpose? Was it to produce energy? Perhaps, but this was not its sole purpose if it were to produce power. The only reason I bring up the idea that it was not the only purpose is that the power theory is incomplete and the method of creating electricity or power involved in Dunn's theory is somewhat incomplete technology, even by today's standards. He is suggesting that the pyramid was a clean energy plant that can pull power from the Earth and transmit it remotely. Although this does seem implausible (even by today's technological proficiencies) I would not discount this idea because we may be close to proving Dunn correct. He may be correct in that one of the pyramid's functions was to produce energy in some way. It may even be through the exact method he has theorized. However, Dunn's theory has not yet come full circle into repeatable experimentation.

What I have done, however, is compile a set of reactions that are repeatable. So to start the reaction process we will need to gain access through the only gate (or entrance) known into the pyramid. This is located at the end of the descending passage. Refer to figure 10 titled "STEP 1." A person carries salt (a.) or a cart filled with salt is attached to a pulley system and lowered into the descending passage to finally reach the Pit area. If the cart is used, the salt is emptied in the Pit and brought back to the surface. Then fresh water is applied (b.) down the passage and it reaches the pit and begins to dissolve the salt. At this point the agitator portion of Cadman's pump can be activated; however, it is not necessary because the salt will eventually dissolve on its own accord (c.).

Once the salt has successfully dissolved into the water the pump system is activated and a system of valves, which most likely have not been excavated yet, are switched and aligned (d.) to allow the salt water solution to reach the King's Chamber southern shaft. When it reaches the southern shaft it is released into the wall of the King's Chamber (e.) and seeps into the Chamber. As previously discussed, in the late 1800's Iron was found in this chamber, and it was shown to have contain gold residue on the outside of it. It either was gold leafed or gold plated at some point. This gold could have a few different uses, which we will discuss later, but the most likely explanation is that it was used as a conductor of electricity. So the "Baghdad" battery technology could have been deployed at this time to activate an electrolysis process within the King's Chamber through use of the shaft system (e.). The shafts could have doubled for two purposes: one would be to transport fluids and gases; two would have been to electrolyze the Chamber via potential gold plating inside the shafts. Or more simply considered, wires could have been run into the chamber using the shafts. All of the above are plausible.

The purpose of electrolyzing the chamber, and thus the salt water solution within the chamber, would be to convert it to Sodium Hydroxide. The by product from this process would, in-turn, be Chlorine gas (f.). The chlorine gas is not waste in this process, so it would be sent up the northern shaft (or back up the southern shaft, but for simplification and flow diagraming - we'll just say it's the northern shaft) and down into a yet discovered holding tank or chamber. At this point some might argue that the UPUAT Project from the 2000's found that the King's Chamber shafts opened to the air. [17] However, to their own admission there were several meters of stones that added layering to the outside surface of the pyramid. This leaves plenty of room for a shaft system to continue and redirect. The only aspect yet discovered would be where it would have reentered the pyramid to reach the Chlorine holding tank. This is not out of the question; because for a long period of time leading up to the UPUAT discovery, we did not know where the King's Chamber shafts exited the pyramid. So we may still yet discover this re-entrance.

## STEP 1

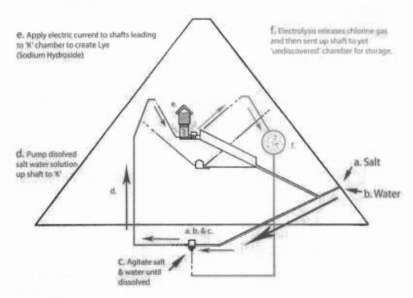

e. Apply electric current to shafts leading to 'X' chamber to create Lye (Sodium Hydroxide)

f. Electrolysis releases chlorine gas and then sent up shaft to yet 'undiscovered' chamber for storage.

d. Pump disolved salt water solution up shaft to 'X'

d.

a. Salt

b. Water

a. b. & c.

C. Agitate salt & water until dissolved

Figure 10

The second stage reaction of the complex is quite a bit simpler and does not even require electrolysis. See figure 11 for reference. Nile water or other fresh water is pumped into the descending passage and flows down into the Pit (a.). It also has been suggested that a wall was built around the pyramid, which acted as a moat and held Nile water up against the pyramid. If this was the case, and the water was also held back by a dike system or gate, then the water could effortlessly be released into the pit instead of pumped. This seems like a more plausible scenario. Read further for a more complete picture of what happens next. Then, a valve in the chamber holding the chlorine gas is opened and it heads through a shaft, or pipe, system and finally connects to the Pit well at the base of the structure (b.). At this point the chlorine gas percolates up through the standing water and the fluid turns into hydrochloric acid during the reaction (c.).

As the Hydrochloric acid reaction winds to a close the valves are shut and the valve system redirects the new flow pattern to the Queen's Chamber (d.). Then the pump system is turned back on and the Pit is evacuated and sends all the Hydrochloric acid away and up to the Queen's Chamber (southern shaft). The Acid now sits in the shaft as it seeps into the chamber and slowly fills it to the desired level. Once the level is reached it now sits in waiting just like the Sodium Hydroxide is now sitting in the King's chamber. It waits for its next move. The Pit is now cleaned by guardians (or a maintenance crew) entering through the descending passage.

Figure 11

## STEP 2

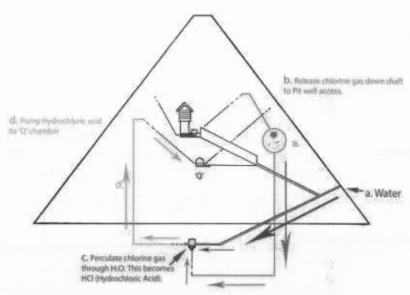

b. Release chlorine gas down shaft to Pit well access.

d. Pump Hydrochloric acid to 'Q' chamber

'Q'

a. Water

C. Perculate chlorine gas through H₂O. This becomes HCl (Hydrochloric Acid).

Now what we have, from the bottom up, is a cleaned Pit, hydrochloric acid in the Queen's Chamber and sodium hydroxide in the King's Chamber. What in the world could this be used for? We begin to answer this question in figure 12. A crew places gold and salt into the Pit area (a.). They then retreat up the descending passage and exit the pyramid. Moat/Nile water is sent flowing into the pit via the descending passage (b.). The solution sits until the salt has completely dissolved in the pit. Now a valve system allows the Queen's Chamber to send some hydrochloric acid out into the ascending passage and it flows down toward the elbow intersection with the descending passage (c.). It flows to the pit and now begins to combine with the salt water and gold. This is enough to begin the reaction, but without an addition of a catalyst this process could take quite some time to dissolve the gold. Yes, contrary to monetary logic, we do want to dissolve the precious gold into suspension. So an answer to this conundrum is the addition of a catalyst. Hydrogen peroxide is the catalyst of choice, which will be explained in the next chapter as to why, and how it is brought in through the pump system. It is brought into the pit via either a yet undiscovered chamber in the pyramid or from outside the pyramid. But nonetheless, it is combined with the hydrochloric acid and gold solution (d.). It slowly reacts until the gold is in complete suspension and appears dissolved. Even with the hydrogen peroxide catalyst, it still could take a few days or even weeks.

Figure 12:

## STEP 3

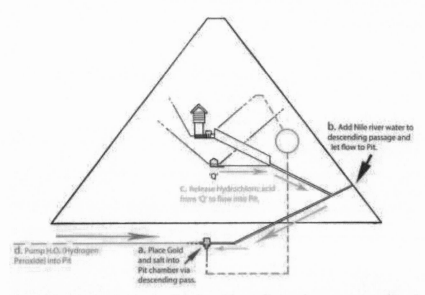

This solution is now a slightly golden yellow substance not unlike the color of honey. The substance in the chamber is now a solution that has a pH of around minus one (-1 pH). It is extremely corrosive and should not sit too long unattended, as well as it is too corrosive for humans to handle. Now it is ready for STEP 4; see figure 13. While the golden solution rests in the Pit, the King's Chamber still has its contents of sodium hydroxide. Sodium hydroxide has a pH of higher than 14 and is extremely basic (14+ pH). The next stage in this process calls for the King's chamber to release some sodium hydroxide into the gallery and to flow down the ascending passage to the elbow intersection of the descending passage and finally come to rest in the Pit to react with the golden solution (a.). What occurs here is a huge swing in pH levels and the goal would be to have it jump into a reaction with sits at 10.78 pH. This will change the color of the solution would change over time to reddish. What is happening is the wild swings in pH are breaking the gold molecules down from its inert large molecule state to smaller and smaller slumps of atoms within the molecules. The next step is to repeat the swing in pH and now add the Queen's Chamber contents (hydrochloric acid) to the Pit and flip the pH back to 1 or less (1 pH) (b.). This breaks down the molecules even more and makes the gold atoms have less and less companions within the molecules. The color of the solution in the pit has now changed colors again to violet. Repeat the flip in pH and now the color has turned to black. Now repeat the pH swing again and now we have a white substance that begins to settle at the bottom of the pit and fluid rises to the top. Each stage may take several days to complete the various reactions. Now that the substance has turned white, feather the contents of the King and Queen's chambers to neutralize the pH to around 7.3 in the Pit (c.).

Allow the white substance to settle for several days. Now activate the pump and let the fluid contents to slowly flow out of the pit as to not disturb the settlement since this white substance is the main reason for the entire series of events. A whitish sludge now remains in the Pit and it is safe to enter since the pH has been neutralized. A crew can now enter the Pit and collect the sludge and place it in a cart for removal. The cart is pulled up the descending passage (d.). The crew then find a flat place with plenty of sunshine, which Egypt has abundant sun, and let it dry into a dry white cake. This cake is now ground into powder for consumption.

Figure 13:

## STEP 4

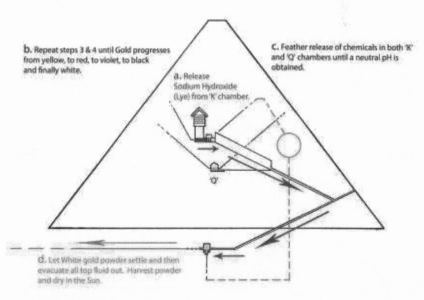

b. Repeat steps 3 & 4 until Gold progresses from yellow, to red, to violet, to black and finally white.

C. Feather release of chemicals in both 'K' and 'Q' chambers until a neutral pH is obtained.

a. Release Sodium Hydroxide (Lye) from 'K' chamber.

'Q'

d. Let White gold powder settle and then evacuate all top fluid out. Harvest powder and dry in the Sun.

What did the Gold turn into? This will be answered in the next chapter.

Why did they consume it? This question is answered within the topics of Part Two in this book.

# 5 WHAT WAS THE END PRODUCT CREATED?

The ancients were making a substance better known today as "monatomic gold." Our understanding of the many uses for this substance is only now resurfacing. Regardless of why this was being consumed or how it may have been used, we must first identify what it actually is. First impressions may discount it but this white powder has gone largely under recognized in modern chemistry. Gold is an inert element and is part of the noble metals group. It does not react with other elements under modern chemical law. Gold does not oxidize, so it is quite novel that this reaction has been successful and can reduce gold into a white powder.

The following excerpt from the Encyclopedia Britannica helps identify the interesting properties of gold:

Gold has several qualities that have made it exceptionally valuable throughout history. It is attractive in colour and brightness, durable to the point of virtual indestructibility, highly malleable, and usually found in nature in a comparatively pure form. The history of gold is unequaled by that of any other metal because of its value in the minds of men from earliest times.

Gold is one of the densest of all metals. It is a good conductor of heat and electricity. It is also soft and the most malleable and ductile of the elements; an ounce (28 grams) can be beaten out to 187 square feet (about 17 square metres) in extremely thin sheets called gold leaf.

Because gold is visually pleasing and workable and does not tarnish or corrode, it was one of the first metals to attract human attention. Examples of elaborate gold workmanship, many in nearly perfect condition, survive from ancient Egyptian, Minoan, Assyrian, and Etruscan artisans, and gold continues to be a highly favoured material out of which to craft jewelry and other decorative objects. (see metalwork; goldwork.)

Because of its unique qualities, gold has been the one material that is universally accepted in exchange for goods and services. In the form of coins or bullion, gold has occasionally played a major role as a high-denomination currency, although silver has generally been the standard medium of payments in the world's trading systems. Gold began to serve as backing for paper-currency systems when they became widespread in the 19th century, and from the 1870s until World War I the gold standard was the basis for the world's currencies. Although gold's official role in the international monetary system had come to an end by the 1970s, the metal remains a highly regarded reserve asset, and approximately 45 percent of all the world's gold is held by governments and central banks for this purpose. Gold is still accepted by all nations as a medium of international payment. (See also money.)

Gold is widespread in low concentrations in all igneous rocks. Its abundance in Earth's crust is estimated at about 0.005 part per million. It occurs mostly in the native state, remaining chemically uncombined except with tellurium, selenium, and possibly bismuth. The element's only naturally occurring isotope is gold-197. Gold often occurs in association with copper and lead deposits, and, though the quantity present is often extremely small, it is readily recovered as a by-product in the refining of those base metals. Large masses of gold-bearing rock rich enough to be called ores are unusual. Two types of deposits containing significant amounts of gold are known: hydrothermal veins, where it is associated with quartz and pyrite (fool's gold); and placer deposits, both consolidated and unconsolidated, that are derived from the weathering of gold-bearing rocks.

Because of its high electrical conductivity (71 percent that of copper) and inertness, the largest industrial use of gold is in the electric and electronics industry for plating contacts, terminals, printed circuits, and semiconductor systems. Thin films of gold that reflect up to 98 percent of incident infrared radiation have been employed on satellites to control temperature and on space-suit visors to afford protection. Used in a similar way on the windows of large office buildings, gold reduces the air-conditioning requirement and adds to the beauty. Gold has also long been used for fillings and other repairs to teeth.

Gold is one of the noblest—that is, least chemically reactive—of the transition elements. It is not attacked by oxygen or sulfur, although it will react readily with halogens or with solutions containing or generating chlorine, such as aqua regia. It also will dissolve in cyanide solutions in the presence of air or hydrogen peroxide. Dissolution in cyanide solutions is attributable to the formation of the very stable dicyanoaurate ion, $[Au(CN)2]-$.

Like copper, gold has a single s electron outside a completed d shell, but, in spite of the similarity in electronic structures and ionization energies, there are few close resemblances between gold on the one hand and copper on the other. [18]

Traditional chemists will say it is not possible to break down gold in the way I have laid out within the Great Pyramid reactions shown earlier. Most of the rationale is identified above from the Encyclopedia Britannica, stating that it is "an inert metal which does not easily breakdown, oxidize or react. It is a noble metal, which should not be broken up without bonding to other chemicals. However, it exists. It can be created."

What is this white powder? It is Mono-Atomic gold. It is gold in a form not completely understood. It is gold, which normally is bunched and bonded in clusters of multiple atoms. Mono-Atomic gold is a state in which the gold bonds are released or broken down, and the individual atoms are allowed to sit free and separate. This appears as a white powder as it is dried.

Here is a repeatable experiment that will allow anyone willing to reduce gold in order to create this unusual white powder.

Here is a recipe I honed that does work and is repeatable. Please be advised, I, the author of this book, am not liable for your choice of making this recipe and take no responsibility of any injury or problem that you may incur by using this recipe. This recipe contains several dangerous chemical reactions and you should take proper precautions prior to and during any handling and/or agitation of any of these chemicals. Perform this operation at your own risk and be sure to adhere to any and all local and federal laws regarding controlled substances and hazardous materials.

***Warning: this reaction contains dangerous chemicals and requires proper eye protection, gloves, closed toed shoes and a lab coat***:

Ingredients:

¼ oz 99.99% Gold leaf or flakes

6oz distilled water

3 teaspoons Salt

8oz Hydrochloric Acid

1oz Hydrogen Peroxide

1 part LYE to 8 Parts water (make around 1 liter total mixture and may not use all)

Equipment:

2 Liter Lab Glass Filtering Flask

Glass stirring wand or wood stirring stick

Process:

1-      Place salt and water into flask and dissolve salt

2-      Place gold into solution

3-      Pour Hydrochloric Acid into flask

4-      Pour small amounts of Hydrochloric acid into flask to slowly dissolve gold into a suspended liquid. Do this slowly by only adding 1/8 of teaspoon at a time and waiting for reaction to die down a bit before the next spoon is added. Wait until gold is completely dissolved in the solution and the liquid looks yellowish. This could take up to 2 weeks.

5-      Add Lye mixture slowly until pH reaches 10.78

6-      Wait until precipitate separates (precipitate turns red) be patient.

7-      Add hydrochloric acid and slowly add Hydrogen peroxide to flip pH back to less than 1 (precipitate turns violet) again patience.

8-      Add Lye until pH reaches 10.78 again (precipitate turns black)

9-      Flip pH again to 1 using step (7) and precipitate turns white. You now have Mono-Atomic Gold.

10-     Neutralize pH to 7.38 and boil solution until it reduces to a sludgy cake. Dry in the sun.

Purists and Alchemists will suggest that you talk to your monoatomic gold powder to insert good energy and good "vibes" as you perform this tedious task.

The following is another recipe developed by Don Nance which also works:

1) Into a 500 ml. flask I place 60 ml. of distilled water.

2) I stir in 1 teaspoon of pure salt. Good to use Morton canning and pickling salt. Be CERTAIN that all of the salt is dissolved and the solution is clear of particulates. This is important. Don't use iodized salt and do not use a salt with anti-caking chemicals in it. Use pure NaCl.

3) Add your gold filings.

4) Stir in, VERY SLOWLY, 80 ml. of muriatic acid. I use ACS quality, but Buckman's Laboratories makes a very pure muriatic, which is available from quality pool/spa

dealers. Smart brand also works. The muriatic must be clear/colorless, as the yellow stuff contains sulfur and will NOT work. The acid must be added VERY slowly. If you go too fast, the salt will precipitate back out of your solution. This will work, but seriously slows down the dissolution of your gold. When this happens, the salt will slowly go back into solution as your gold dissolves. So if this occurs, just go on with the recipe, realizing that it slowed you down considerably.

5) Add in some 35% $H2O2$ (hydrogen peroxide) food grade or technical grade (minimum). Add it about 1 teaspoon at a time and wait 20 minutes. A "fire" will begin inside of your flask. You want to have a good steady stream of bubbles coming from all of your gold. You also want to build your fire slowly. If you add too much $H2O2$ you run the risk of having it boil on you and it will come out of your flask and the gassing will be extreme and acid will go everywhere and life on our planet, as we know it, will have changed ;-)

6) Place this inside of a shield (nest) and check it three times a day. Add $H2O2$ as needed until your gold goes away. This takes as long as it takes. The Philosophers had many ways of marking time. The two that we are concerned with here are the lunar phases and the "elastic" time, that which is marked by a reaction taking as long as it takes. The variable being that you will never have exactly the same particle size for your gold and the phase of the moon. Best to do your dissolution during the waning moon and precipitations during the waxing, culminating during the full moon. Believe it or not, this really makes a difference.

7) Once all of your gold is dissolved, add more $H2O2$ and keep the fire going for a while longer. This will help to break up the metallic clusters.

Once this is complete, you will have a very pretty gold chloride. Its ph will be MINUS 2.0 (on my well-calibrated meter). It will eat you to the bone. Always wear protection for eyes, hands, etc...anything that you could not stand to lose :)

From here there are several "ways to go." The most direct way to white gold is to make up a lye menstruum of about 1 part lye to 8 parts water. This is about 18 oz. of lye crystals slowly dissolved into a gallon of distilled water.

This reaction creates heat and some nasty fumes and needs to be done in a glass jar or beaker. The lye, just like the acids, are always added to the water. NEVER add water to concentrated lye or to concentrated acid. You will have a big problem!

8) Once your gold solution has stopped bubbling from the H2O2, begin dripping your 1/8 lye menstruum into it at a rate of about 4 drops per second while stirring briskly. You ARE wearing gloves and eye protection, aren't you? You really don't need a ph meter for this. Just bring the ph up but not too quickly! If you do it too fast, it will boil on you...if you see some steam collecting on the sides of your flask, you are getting too hot. Slow down your lye addition and keep stirring. This reaction takes a WHILE.

Your solution will clear, you can stop and rest here. If you are going too fast, the solution will clear and then very quickly change color and a precipitate will form. That's fine, no worries.

Stop adding lye when you get a precipitate, this will occur by ph 10.78 if you are using a meter. If no meter, stop when you get a color change and a precipitate.

While you are resting, mix up an acid solution in a glass jar by adding 4 parts of muriatic acid to 3 parts of distilled water.

9) Start stirring your gold solution and slowly drip in some of this acid solution. This acid solution should approximate a 20% strength. Stop adding acid solution when your gold precipitate disappears. The ph will be around ph 1 or so. The color of the solution will likely be gold but not as concentrated looking as before. It may also be another color. No worries - again, just look at it to see that there are no particles. If so, add more acid solution. If you still have particles, stop there and add some more H2O2 just as before and break it up some more.

10) Begin stirring your gold acid solution and start dropping in your LYE menstruum to again raise the ph of your solution. You want to go on up to ph 10.78 again or until you get a precipitate. Don't be surprised if this is yet a different color from the last time you did this.

11) Now bring the ph back down into acid using your 20% HCL solution that you likely made from muriatic acid. This time, when the particles disappear, the solution will no longer be gold colored at all. This is your clue that

the metal bonds are broken up sufficiently to proceed.

12) Now, Bring the ph of your solution up to about ph 8.0 or so by stirring quickly and adding your lye menstruum in drops.

12a) let the precipitate settle well, then pour off the top water and KEEP it, (You can evaporate this down, very slowly, and obtain a white powder of gold trichloride which is VERY POTENT) and wash the precipitate with 3 times as much distilled water as you have precipitate by volume. This is done by simply adding the Universal Solvent (distilled water) to your separated precipitate and stirring. You let this settle and pour it off (I eat it :) then add the original top water back into the precipitate...then proceed to the next step...or you can skip all of step 12a and just jump right to...

13) Place the precipitate and top water into a boiling flask and over a gas flame or candle, slowly evaporate the water from your precipitate. My advice is to not boil this and go to a just-dry state. This, again, takes as long as it takes. Do not boil it, and do not bake the dryness or scorch it. You want it just thoroughly dry. The addition of the gentle heat will help the oils reunite with the precipitate. Boiling it will drive off m-state.

14) Once it is thoroughly dry, you will need to get a large boiling pot. I use a Visions glass/ceramic dutch oven in 5 quart size WITH LID. Boiling won't drive off so much of the m-state now that the oils are reunited with the precipitate. Take it out of doors, on a moonlit night, before the full moon, and place your dry precipitate inside of it. In a separate glass jar, add 18 ounces of lye slowly into 1 gallon of distilled water. This causes heat and must be thoroughly stirred in until it clears. Don't breathe the vapors.

15) Stir this now clear lye menstruum into your boiling pot with your precipitate sitting there.

16) Bring this to a full rolling boil and reduce the heat, while stirring, then cover tightly and place a brick or some other inflammable weight on the lid to reduce steam losses. THIS BOILING LYE IS VERY VERY VERY DANGEROUS!!! Let it boil, at a gentle rolling boil, for at least 4 hours.

17) When done, add some distilled water to bring the level back up to one gallon. Let it cool and settle.

18) Filter your solution through unbleached filters until it is clear of any particulates. I use a 1 micron filtering system.

19) While stirring your filtered solution rapidly, drip in some of your 20% HCL solution (acid solution) to reduce the ph to around 8.0 .

If you want to get fancy, go down slowly (all of this step is done SLOWLY) to below 2 ph and then add some of your 1/8 lye menstruum to bring the ph back up to 7.8 ph.

20) Let your white precipitate settle and separate the top water from it and save the top water.

21) Wash the precipitate as before in distilled water. Let it settle and separate. Save this top water.

At this point you can marry the top water to the precipitate by evaporation, as before, or you can simply dry the white, saltless precipitate and anneal it or you can measure it into water and have at it. [19]

The following website illustrates an unidentified person's recipe (note: it may be hard to understand but it does allow you to see each stage of the process quite thoroughly). I do recommend watching it in order to get a visual understanding of the process:[20]
http://www.youtube.com/watch?v=nm8IKtIhMnI

The above representations are just three varieties of making mono-atomic gold from scratch. There are many more methods to making this white powder. In fact, there is a group of people who call themselves "Alchemists," and they take the process very seriously. They tend to make up their own recipes and rituals regarding the creation of this substance and some guard their recipes closely. I am actually surprised to find the recipes I did. Nonetheless, they work and are repeatable. In addition - I am taking this mono-atomic gold as I write this book. In the following portion we will examine the reasons for consuming mono-atomic gold and the potential theological significance of this white powder.

# PART TWO:

## THE SIGNIFICANCE OF MONO-ATOMIC GOLD

## &

## WHY THE GLOBAL ELITE DOES NOT WANT US TO USE IT

## 6 MONO-ATOMIC GOLD FOUND IN THE PAST

The Torah, the Bible's Old Testament, New Testament and ancient Sumerian texts all hold hints and mentions of an important white powder of some sort. This white powder is described many ways throughout these ancient texts. It is called powder and manna in The Book of Exodus. It's described as milk and honey from the heavens. It's called Sho-Bread. It has many names. However, identifying all forms of this substance requires circumstantial evidence tying them together. This is because, for reasons beyond our current understanding, the authors of these texts were quite coded and cryptic in writing about most of the spiritual guidance. Parables are rampant, if not all encompassing, within the Torah and the Bible. This is quite possibly for its own protection. Being cryptic regarding this subject might actually be the very reason for its survival. I say this because it has become apparent in recent years that many books of the original bible were omitted and edited heavily in order to shield readers from understanding the truth about our past. For this reason, care is taken in extracting these key words and assuring they really mean what they are intended to mean. Although much of the Bible, not unlike the pyramids themselves, is multi-layered in meaning, only one layer is needed to show enough evidence that the authors of the Bible are talking about mono-atomic gold in many places.

Let's take a look at some references to manna first and see if there might be some correlation:

Deuteronomy 8:3 ESV - And he humbled you and let you hunger and fed you with manna, which you did not know, nor did your fathers know, that he might make you know that man does not live by bread alone, but man lives by every word that comes from the mouth of the Lord. Exodus 16:35 ESV - The people of Israel ate the manna forty years, till they came to a habitable land. They ate the manna till they came to the border of the land of Canaan. Exodus 16:1-36 ESV - They set out from Elim, and all the congregation of the people of Israel came to the wilderness of Sin, which is between Elim and Sinai, on the fifteenth day of the second month after they had departed from the land of Egypt. And the whole congregation of the people of Israel grumbled against Moses and Aaron in the wilderness, and the people of Israel said to them, "Would that we had died by the hand of the Lord in the land of Egypt, when we sat by the meat pots and ate bread to the full, for you have brought us out into this wilderness to kill this whole assembly with hunger." Then the Lord said to Moses, "Behold, I am about to rain bread from heaven for you, and the people shall go out and gather a day's portion every day, that I may test them, whether they will walk in my law or not. On the sixth day, when they prepare what they bring in, it will be twice as much as they gather daily." [21]

We see here in Exodus and Deuteronomy that the Israelites were either eating manna on their own accord, suggested to eat manna, or forced to eat manna. This is quite significant because it not only appeared to be a potential supplement; it seems that it is treated as a replacement for food. Why would they eat it? Not only did they eat it, but according to Moses they ate it for 40 years until they reached Canaan. That is a long time to eat only manna or to highlight the consumption of manna even if they ate other food. That is, if it is "food" at all. But it must not be a previously considered type of food because the Israelites also complain in Exodus 16:1-36 about it not being meat and bread like they were eating their fill of in Egypt before the Exodus. This could mean two things: one - they were fasting except for the consumption of manna and water or; two- it means they were eating manna during this period in addition to other food. I tend to think they were fasting due to the mention of Israelites complaining. If it were a supplement, I don't think they would have complained about the addition of another intake. However, if they longed for the past and wished they could have opulence again, this suggests that something was taken away. This is why I believe they were fasting. So what in the world is this substance? Can it be manufactured as we would need to see? A great culprit for evidence of manufacturing of the manna would be when Moses melted the golden calf in Exodus 32:

1 When the people saw that Moses was so long in coming down from the mountain, they gathered around Aaron and said, "Come, make us gods who will go before us. As for this fellow Moses who brought us up out of Egypt, we don't know what has happened to him."

2 Aaron answered them, "Take off the gold earrings that your wives, your sons and your daughters are wearing, and bring them to me." 3 So all the people took off their earrings and brought them to Aaron. 4 He took what they handed him and made it into an idol cast in the shape of a calf, fashioning it with a tool. Then they said, "These are your gods, Israel, who brought you up out of Egypt."

5 When Aaron saw this, he built an altar in front of the calf and announced, "Tomorrow there will be a festival to the Lord."

6 So the next day the people rose early and sacrificed burnt offerings and presented fellowship offerings. Afterward they sat down to eat and drink and got up to indulge in revelry.

7 Then the Lord said to Moses, "Go down, because your people, whom you brought up out of Egypt, have become corrupt.

8 They have been quick to turn away from what I commanded them and have made themselves an idol cast in the shape of a calf. They have bowed down to it and sacrificed to it and have said, 'These are your gods, Israel, who brought you up out of Egypt.'

9 "I have seen these people," the Lord said to Moses, "and they are a stiff-necked people.

10 Now leave me alone so that my anger may burn against them and that I may destroy them. Then I will make you into a great nation."

11 But Moses sought the favor of the Lord his God. "Lord," he said, "why should your anger burn against your people, whom you brought out of Egypt with great power and a mighty hand?

12 Why should the Egyptians say, 'It was with evil intent that he brought them out, to kill them in the mountains and to wipe them off the face of the earth'? Turn from your fierce anger; relent and do not bring disaster on your people.

13 Remember your servants Abraham, Isaac and Israel, to whom you swore by your own self: 'I will make your descendants as numerous as the stars in the sky and I will give your descendants all this land I promised them, and it will be their inheritance forever.'"

14 Then the Lord relented and did not bring on his people the disaster he had threatened.

15 Moses turned and went down the mountain with the two tablets of the covenant law in his hands. They were inscribed on both sides, front and back.

16 The tablets were the work of God; the writing was the writing of God, engraved on the tablets.

17 When Joshua heard the noise of the people shouting, he said to Moses, "There is the sound of war in the camp."

18 Moses replied: "It is not the sound of victory, it is not the sound of defeat; it is the sound of singing that I hear."

19 When Moses approached the camp and saw the calf and the dancing, his anger burned and he threw the tablets out of his hands, breaking them to pieces at the foot of the mountain.

20 And he took the calf the people had made and burned it in the fire; then he ground it to powder, scattered it on the water and made the Israelites drink it.

21 He said to Aaron, "What did these people do to you, that you led them into such great sin?"

22 "Do not be angry, my lord," Aaron answered. "You know how prone these people are to evil.

23 They said to me, 'Make us gods who will go before us. As for this fellow Moses who brought us up out of Egypt, we don't know what has happened to him.'

24 So I told them, 'Whoever has any gold jewelry, take it off.' Then they gave me the gold, and I threw it into the fire, and out came this calf!"

25 Moses saw that the people were running wild and that Aaron had let them get out of control and so become a laughingstock to their enemies.

26 So he stood at the entrance to the camp and said, "Whoever is for the Lord, come to me." And all the Levites rallied to him.

27 Then he said to them, "This is what the Lord, the God of Israel, says: 'Each man strap a sword to his side.

Go back and forth through the camp from one end to the other, each killing his brother and friend and neighbor.'"

28 The Levites did as Moses commanded, and that day about three thousand of the people died.

29 Then Moses said, "You have been set apart to the Lord today, for you were against your own sons and brothers, and he has blessed you this day."

30 The next day Moses said to the people, "You have committed a great sin. But now I will go up to the Lord; perhaps I can make atonement for your sin."

31 So Moses went back to the Lord and said, "Oh, what a great sin these people have committed! They have made themselves gods of gold.

32 But now, please forgive their sin—but if not, then blot me out of the book you have written."

33 The Lord replied to Moses, "Whoever has sinned against me I will blot out of my book.

34 Now go, lead the people to the place I spoke of, and my angel will go before you. However, when the time comes for me to punish, I will punish them for their sin."

35 And the Lord struck the people with a plague because of what they did with the calf Aaron had made. [22]

In Exodus 20, Moses burned the golden calf in the fire. This could be interpreted in two ways: He could have literally burned it in the fire, or he could have performed the chemical process laid out in part one of this book. For all intents and purposes a smoldering steam could look like smoke. The process of making monoatomic gold does fume quite a bit. It fumes enough to make one have to do it outside.

The next important detail to point out in Exodus 20 is that Moses then grounded the melted gold into a powder. This is highly unlikely because gold will melt, but it is so soft and malleable that it has a tendency to stick and cake up on whatever is trying to break it up. It naturally likes to stick to itself and the item that is trying to break it up... similar to lead. They are most likely grinding up dried monoatomic gold here.

Then Moses has them consume it. He mixes it with water and makes them drink it. What in the world would anyone do that for; why would anyone eat ground up gold powder? Why was it necessary to melt the gold, grind it up into a powder, mix it with water and often drink it? Couldn't they have just carved pieces of the gold off of the calf and gournd it up that way? That is the dead giveaway here for me. For Moses to melt the gold before grinding it accomplishes nothing different than what Aaron already did. Aaron had previously melted all the jewelry and made a calf out of it.

Moses must have noticed that Aaron did something wrong in attempting to achieve the desired result. If all Aaron did was melt the gold and let it harden, then what did Moses do differently? Moses performed a completely different task. Although it is shown as a fire, which melted the calf, maybe it was something completely different. Maybe the word for chemically breaking down the gold into a different substance was lost in translation? If not, then the only thing Moses did was re-melt the exact same gold which Aaron melted previously. Nothing would have changed here, so it is obvious that a chemical process was the chief differentiating factor between Moses's act and Aaron's act. Aaron could have possibly watched Moses do this before, but not know the entire process. That seems to be the most likely scenario here. Aaron probably did not understand or learn the proper chemical process, so he just imitated what he saw Moses do and was unsuccessful.

Now it bares revisiting the book of Exodus mentioning the "wilderness of Sin:" "Exodus 16:1-36 ESV – "They set out from Elim, and all the congregation of the people of Israel came to the wilderness of Sin, which is between Elim and Sinai, on the fifteenth day of the second month after they had departed from the land of Egypt." This catches my attention because there is another text that discusses this "land of Sin or Wilderness of Sin." This would be the Sumerian tablets. If you look at the spelling of Elim and Sinai, it is not too far of a stretch of linguistics to make a comparison to some of the Sumerian characters. Since neither of these texts were originally written in the English language, one can only assume we are phonetically recording these names for proper pronunciation. In his extension of Zachariah Zichin's research, Gerald Clark identifies some culprits which help us understand what, or even who, reigns over this land of Sin or Sinai and their starting point of Elim. Clark marks this significant finding in his book, *The Annunaki of Nibiru* noted below:

> A female Sumerian deity, Inanna, was also known as Hathor in Egypt and her name is well recognized and memorialized on the walls of temples to include the Temple of Hathor found on Mount Serabit El Khadim, the Biblical Mount Sinai; the mountain in the wilderness of the deity Nannar-Sin. The deity Sin is also described in various traditions to include Assyria, and those cultures that associate with the crescent moon symbol found on flags and mosques affiliated with the religion of Islam. The male deity recognized as the moon god to the peoples of Mesopotamia was Nannar-Sin who also had a sister, none other than the goddess Inanna aka Hathor to the Egyptians. From the genealogy accounts inscribed in baked clay on display in museums throughout the world

the authors readily proclaimed in the Sumerian records, Nannar-Sin was the son of Enlil, and was also known as the moon god to peoples of the ancient Middle East. [23]

Now Clark does not delve into the relationship between Elim and Enlil, but I would venture to say it is quite possible that these two words could have been one and the same, originally. If some zealous gods or entities held themselves in high regard, they might have called the land in that they reigned supreme by their own name. So the wilderness of Sin could have been the land that was reigned and ruled by Nannar-Sin and the land of Elim, or maybe Enlil could have been named after himself as well. So Moses could have taken his people from the land of Enlil, through the wilderness of Sin and finally came to rest in Canaan. This recognition of wilderness of Sin and its relationship to Nannar-Sin, and thus Mount Sinai, is significant because these gods of the Sumerian texts were in pursuit of a substance that is relavent to this work. The Sumerian gods, which the humans of Sumer called the Annunaki, had an appetite for gold. And the idea of the Annunaki and their short background are noted below:

According to the interpretations of Sumerologists , the term AN.UNNA.KI literally is interpreted as those who from "heaven to earth came." The key point to note early on is the affiliation of the term "Heaven" with the claimed planet of Anunnaki origin, namely Nibiru as detailed in "The 12th Planet," written by Sitchin in 1976. Additionally, from the list of characters detailed as "deities" in Mesopotamian literature like the "Epic of Gilgamesh", we know that the head of the Anunnaki council of 12 was chaired by Anu, the father of the two key players and half brothers Enlil and Enki. [24]

The Sumerians revered Anu as being the main leader (or father), and Enlil and Enki were identified as being the Sumerians main entities through which they interacted. Clark also highlights the fact that the ancient Sumerians understood that their home in the heavens was not just heaven, but a planet called Nibiru. And as these gods or reigning entities came to Earth, they came to Earth from Nibiru (which was considered Heaven by the gods, not by the people). So the people mainly copied the longing that the gods held and called Nibiru "Heaven" as well, "Equating the planet Nibiru with the word Heaven, as used in the Bible, is an important detail when re-examining prayers like "Our Father who art in Heaven...", shining a whole new light on who the Father in Heaven actually was, namely Anu. Thus the prayer must have originated among one of his kids on Earth, Enlil, Enki, or Ninmah or Ninharsag..." [25]

But what did they (the gods) really want with us and the Earth? That is the real question. If they created us, they must have had big plans for our purpose. First we'll look at the reason they came to Earth:

What was the reason that the Anunnaki left Nibiru to come to the Earth? Nibiru, located beyond Pluto in our Solar System, is trapped in a 3600-year retrograde elliptical orbit around our sun. According to maps found in Sumer, and reports from the 1986 IRAS Naval Observatory discovery of a brown dwarf in the region Nibiru was reported to reside by the Sumerians, and the intense Catholic focus on Mount Graham using the L.U.C.I.F.E.R. scope watching for Nibiru's arrival, the planet is real. So, what prompted an advanced civilization on Nibiru to send a team of exploratory scientists to Earth? ...various political struggles for power were ongoing with environmental pressures garnering the attention of the governing council on Nibiru.

Consider the periodic exposure of an outer planet that normally receives very low levels of direct solar radiation in its outer orbit but intense exposure during the close perigee when the atmosphere would receive a larger radiation dose. According to Sitchin's published history timeline [88] approximately 450,000 years ago, life on Nibiru was facing extinction due to a deteriorating atmosphere and the subsequent exposure to radiation, especially at close perigee with the sun.

Alalu [a fallen dictator losing to Anu] escapes in a space craft in anticipation of his exile sentencing and subsequently discovers *gold on Earth*. Alalu's precious metal discovery is offered as an amend to save Nibiru's failing atmosphere by *dispersing ionized gold particles* into the home planet's degrading atmosphere. [26]

Much of what is learned by Alalu is taken to heart by the home planet. The Annunaki take this task of extracting gold from Earth very seriously. In fact, they take it so seriously that they immediately sent teams of lower class Annunaki, called Igigi, to Earth to mine for gold. At first, according to Zitchin and Clark, they are able to quite easily extract it Gold from the ocean water around the Saudi Arabian peninsula and the Persian Gulf head waters. This is because the dry air in that region of the ocean keeps the mineral level high. It has less fresh water in its composition, so it is easier to remove the water and extract the minerals and thus the gold.

However, although this method is quite simple the Annunaki on Nibiru are growing restless and impatient . This is because the method is slow. They can't keep up with the growing demand because the radiation problem [they claim] is getting worse. So as the home planet asks for the gold faster, Enki and Enlil realize they must do something different. "The higher ranking members of the Anunnaki Council, purportedly Enki himself, brought several subservient workers to help with establishing the gold mining outpost on Earth. The Lost Book of Enoch refers to them as Watchers [36], but the Atrahasis calls the miners "Igigi." They were apparently very advanced, (relative to humans) although designated the working class agent." [27] And the following passage explains where they decided to mine for the gold on land, where it is known to be in higher concentrations:

The mining operation was being transitioned from the waters of the Persian Gulf to mining the ore located by Enki in South Africa, in the vicinity of the Zambezi River. Given the support infrastructure that would be needed to crush rock and process gold-laden ore, Enki and Enlil invited Anu to come to Earth and provide council on the arduous mining task.

According to the Atrahasis [*which according to Clark is the same person we would know as Noah and his story in the Torah and Old Testament*] account, Anu, Enlil, and Enki drew lots to determine which mission each would pursue separately, creating space between the two half brothers that were often at odds. Enki was the first born son to Anu and Antu. Enlil was, according to the Sumerian accounts, the rightful heir. Based on Niburian inheritance rules, the rightful heir is designated as the offspring of the male and his half -sister. The reason this was done by the Anunnaki was rooted in science. The female contribution to the genetic material includes mitochondrial DNA which the male does not. This predisposes the genetic blood line toward the maternal source.

Following the drawing of lots, Enlil was assigned to the Mesopotamian region where he would eventually be served by Terah and his son Abram [*name look familiar?*] in the temple at Ur. Enki was assigned to the Abzu (Africa ) to speed up the gold mining operation badly needed to repair the Niburian degenerating atmosphere. Anu returned to Nibiru to run the kingship back on the home planet. Innana, Anu's favorite granddaughter, was given the Indus Valley region, and the **Sinai Peninsula** was retained for use by the Anunnaki. The division took place and was finalized in the calendar year 3760 BCE. [28]

When we see that the Annunaki preserved the Sinai peninsula to be for their personal use, it would be expected that evidence of their presence would be found as Moses led the Israelites through the wilderness of Sin. The Israelite were able to just gather Manna from the ground, which was in areas of Sinai as the Annunaki would have had it on hand and about the area. This Manna was described as "milk and honey" of the heavens. In fact, they were said to be travelling through an area the Israelites called "the Land of Milk and Honey." This would be aptly named for a place the Annunaki used for themselves, especially since they were not only sending this gold back to Heaven or Nibiru. but they were also consuming it to help repair themselves. "There were complaints from the Anunnaki about noticeable aging effects that were not seen on Nibiru . It was postulated that the more rapid circuits they were experiencing on Earth versus Nibiru with a much slower circuit, namely a 3,600 year 'shar.'" [29] So at this point, we would assume that they either left the planet or created a remedy to this aging process. Would they have benefitted from the consumption of the same element, which they were taking home to Nibiru, Gold? It does seem fitting.

The Torah and the Bible talk about the Israelites consuming Shewbread (also known as showbread or sho-bread). What is shewbread and where do we see it?

Within the Torah, the shewbread is mentioned exclusively by the Priestly Code and Holiness Code, but certain sections of the Bible, including the Book of Chronicles, Books of Samuel, and Book of Kings, also describe aspects of them. In the Holiness Code, the shewbread is described as twelve cakes/loaves baked from fine flour, arranged in two rows/piles on a table standing before God; each loaf/cake was to contain two Omers of flour (Leviticus 24:5-6). The Biblical regulations specify that cups of frankincense were to be placed upon the rows of cakes, and the Septuagint, but not the masoretic text, states that salt was mixed with the frankincense; the frankincense, which the Septuagint refers to as an anamnesis, (a hapax legomenon), constituted a memorial (azkarah), having been offered upon the altar to God (Leviticus 24:7-9).

According to the Book of Chronicles, the Kohathite clan had charge of the baking and setting in order of the bread, suggesting that there were secret extra requirements in preparing the bread, known only to the Kohathites. Since leavened products were prohibited from the altar, and the cakes/loaves are not described as being offered upon it, it is possible that the shewbread was leavened; however, as they were carried into the inner part of the sanctuary, it is highly probable that they were unleavened.

The cakes were to be left on the table for a week, and then be replaced with new ones on the Sabbath, so that there were always fresh loaves on the table, and those that had started going stale were removed; the Biblical text states that the Jewish priests were entitled to eat the cakes that had been removed, as long as they did so in a holy place, as it considered the bread to be holy. It appears that consumption of the bread wasn't the exclusive preserve of the priests, as the narrative of David's sojourn at Nob mentions that Ahimelek (the priest) gave David the holy bread, at his request. [30]

In this description there are a few things that are only touched upon, which must be not only identified, but explained in further detail. This is because the Bible and Torah are notorious for one–liners, which leave the reader wanting more. One thing that is identified in this Showbread presentation is the use of Frankincense. Why use frankincense? What is so significant about Frankincense? Frankincense is also used in meditation to help open the pineal gland or third eye chakra:

[Frankincense is] sometimes called olibanum. This sweet protector of the heavens operates far beyond the auric field, in the light realms. It is adaptogenic—it will adapt to a person's spiritual state of being. Holding the wisdom of the ages, it waits for what is asked of it, and can do all that may be required. If it encounters malevolent energies attached to a person, it has the authority and power to assist in the removal of all that is unwanted.

In the cases of spiritual shock or loss, when the spirit can step out of the body, Frankincense can gently ease us back to our earthly home.

Frankincense helps each of us connect to that part of ourselves which is eternal and divine. It is one of the most ancient of the incenses, having been in use for at least 3,000 years.

Frankincense increases oxygenation, which increases the life force in the physical body. Frankincense has the ability to deepen and slow the breath and this helps to bring the body and mind into a meditative state. It helps break ties with the past, especially when they block personal growth. Use it in baths with the conscious intention of "washing away" any old ties which feel like a hindrance.

[It is] an important oil for anointing the dying and keeping the soul connected to its divine essence. It is excellent for the Sixth Chakra [3r eye or pineal gland], assisting in altering perception of truth and promoting clairvoyance. The Crown and Heart Chakras also expand as new realities are perceived. The light body enlarges as new realities and dimensions are experienced. It can help with memory. It opens the 3rd Eye for connection.

The Hebrew word for frankincense, levonah (sometimes translated as "incense"), is mentioned in the Bible 22 times and referenced indirectly another 59 times. 'Who is this that cometh out of the wilderness like pillars of smoke, perfumed with myrrh and frankincense with all powders of the merchant?' (Song of Solomon 3:6) [31]

This helps put the importance of frankincense into perspective. Since we are discussing a holistic approach to understanding how gold mining was a global phenomenon, it is also necessary to tie in a global perspective when understanding what it may have been used for and how it may have been prepared and displayed. But why would a multi-dimensional facet, stemming from the Frankincense, be important for the Shewbread? The next significant item has the shewbread on an alter for God (or is it gods?). This would help identify for who the shewbread was prepared. You will also know that the priests are allowed to consume this bread after it has been set for 7 days. So this is also a good moment to point out that the priests would have been receiving the benefit of the shewbread ingredients.

Another interesting side note, which is only hinted at in the Bible and the Torah, is that the main portion of the recipe was secret and only known by the Kohathites. This means that other ingredients, which are also significant enough to be placed on the alter to God, are being secretly added into the mixture. This secret is important. Maybe if we ask the question of "who were, or are, the Kohathites?," then maybe we can get closer to discovering these secret ingredients, or ingredient. The Kohathites were in charge of bringing God's presence to Earth. Can this be a mention of a multidimensional substance straddling two dimensions, that of Earthly man and godly or heavenly beings?

Kohath was the second son of Levi and grandfather of *Moses, *Aaron, and *Miriam (Num. 26:58–59). Few personal details about him are recorded. He is invariably listed between his brothers Gershon and Merari (Gen. 46:11; Ex. 6:16; Num. 3:17; I Chron. 5:27). He lived for 133 years and had four sons: Amram, Izhar, Hebron, and Uzziel (Ex. 6:18). The information about his descendants is more detailed, since the Kohathites were among the most important levitical clans. Their story is interwoven with four periods in biblical history – the Wilderness Wanderings, the Settlement, the Monarchy, and the Return to Zion. In the census taken in the wilderness the Kohathites numbered 8,600 males (LXX, 8,300) aged above one month, including 2,750 males between 30 and 50 years old (Num. 3:28; 4:1–3, 34–37). They were subject to service for work relating to the Tent of Meeting. They camped along the south side of the Tabernacle and were in charge of the most sacred objects, the Ark, the table, the lampstand, the altars, the sacred utensils, and the screen, all of which they carried on their shoulders. The sons of Kohath were granted a privilege greater than that awarded to the other clans of the Levites, the Gershonites and the Merarites, in that they bore their burden on staves, unlike others who carried them on ox wagons (Num. 3:29, 31; 4:2, 7:8–9). Another episode which relates to the wilderness period was the rebellion by *Korah, grandson of Kohath, against the leadership of Moses and Aaron (Num. 16:1ff.). The details about the allotted settlements of the Kohathites are given in Joshua (21:4–5, 9–26) and I Chronicles (6:39–46). Those descended from Aaron received 13 towns within the tribal territories of Judah, Simon, and Benjamin. The remaining Kohathites received ten additional towns from the tribes of Ephraim, Dan, and half of Manasseh. Their allotted lands were thus mainly in the southern and central parts of the country. In the Chronicler's reconstruction of the period of the monarchy the Kohathites are mentioned in connection with the four kings – David, Hezekiah, Jehoshaphat, and Josiah, always in relation to service in the Tabernacle or the Temple. According to Chronicles, it was during David's reign, that the family of Heman the Kohathite was among the levites assigned to direct the singing in the Tabernacle (I Chron. 6:16–23; cf. Ps. 88:1). Led by Uriel "the Chief," 120 Kohathites participated in the installation of the Ark in Jerusalem (I Chron. 15:5), and the family is again listed in the census of Levites and their organization in divisions is undertaken by David (I Chron. 23:1–6, 12). Another tradition in Chronicles reports that in the days of King Jehoshaphat, during the invasion of Judah by the Moabites and Ammonites, it was the Kohathites who led the congregation in praise of God at the service of intercession (II Chron. 20:19). They also participated in the cleansing of the Temple in the time of Hezekiah (II Chron. 29:12), and two of their men supervised the work of renovating the Temple undertaken by King Josiah (II Chron. 34:12). In the era of the return to Zion, the time of Ezra and Nehemiah, when functions were determined in the Temple, several of the sons of Kohath were put in charge of the changing of the showbread (I Chron. 9:32). [Nili Shupak]

In the Aggadah

Kohath was one of the seven righteous men who helped bring the Shekhinah, the Divine Presence, back to earth, after it had ascended to heaven because of the sins of previous generations (PdRK, I, 22). Because of the superiority of the family of Kohath among the families of the tribe of Levi they were given the privilege of carrying the Ark in the wilderness. The diminution in numbers which this caused the family of Kohath (cf. Num. 4:18–19) was due to the fact that a fire emerged from the Ark, which occasionally destroyed those who carried it, and from the deaths which occurred as a result of the frantic desire of members of the family to be granted the privilege (Gen. R. 5:1). Their humility is praised. "Although the family of Kohath were aristocrats, when they came to carry the ark, they assumed the demeanor of ordinary slaves"; they carried the ark on their shoulders, while walking backward, as a sign of respect (Gen. R. 5:8). [32]

The Kohathites were identified as aristocrats among Moses' people. This also hints at the idea that they literally would "go-between" for the gods and men. Were they in charge of the divine substance that the gods craved? It does certainly seem that way. They were involved in the gathering of manna in the wilderness and were present with Moses when he reduced the gold to a white powder. Were they the ones who knew how to "alchemize" the gold into a white powder and/or either showed Moses how to perform this task? Or were they the ones to actually preformed the task and presented it to Moses? Either way, it is a fascinating concept that they are the guardians of this secret ingredient. For many generations, these Kohathites were the guardians of this secret. Tradition is not lost in the Hebrew world. This is evident in how the Torah is actually transcribed. This being said I would venture to say this practice of keeping the addition of manna or white powder gold to the shewbread was practiced for centuries, if not still practiced. So it seems as though the Kohathites were the guardians of the white powder and were also allowed to consume it as a gift from the gods, or shall we say Annunaki, for providing them with the substance of their perpetual youth and planet shielding material. It is hard to believe that the Kohathites really had enough gold on hand to provide for the shielding of an entire planet, but they could have had plenty for the creation of monoatomic gold, and thus the consumption thereof.

So if the Kohathites were considered the aristocratic gatekeepers of the monoatomic gold, or at least of gold, then they would have been the leaders of the priesthood. Kohathites were the true priest class. All extra-dimensional activity went through them within the Hebrew world. So what happened to the priest class we would know as the Kohathites? This is really a loaded question. But before we answer that question, in the last chapter we should investigate what some of the known purposes and uses of mono-atomic gold are. But one civilization, specifically the ancient Egyptians, could have been actively creating monoatomic gold regularly as we discussed earlier by examining the chemical reaction theory within the Great Pyramid.

Regardless if it can be proven that the Egyptians, as we know them today through the hieroglyphic records, actually were the culprits in the building of the Great Pyramid, I feel strongly that it must be recognized that they were actually using the Pyramid as a functioning device. Dunn likes to call them "the guardians" in his work. This is an appropriate label, I believe.

There are many reliefs carved throughout Egypt that depict the offering and consumption of something they called, "MFKZT" or translated into "what is it?" This can be seen first in a photograph of a carving called the "The Inscriptions of Sinai" here in figure 14:

Figure 14

This stone shows a relief from the 18th dynasty and the following drawing highlights the markings a bit more clearly in figure 15:

Figure 15

Above is the usual winged disk, below it on the right Hatshepsut as king offers white bread to Anhur-Show, and, on the left, Tuthmosis III presents wine to Hathor, lady of the turquoise. Date: 'Year 20'.

Below the scene are eleven horizontal lines of inscription, of which the last three are shortened on the left to admit a standing figure of Nakht.

'The scribe Nakhi, he says: I followed the good god, for the lord of the two lands knew that I was excellent, I walking on the road and being honoured on account of it (?), the officials of the palace bending the arm before me. The Horus himself sent me to do what his spirit desired. He promoted (?) me and I was foremost among millions of men, having been sought among hundreds of thousands of men. He appointed me royal envoy, I being exalted [before] the (other) courtiers, for Hathor, lady of the turquoise, showed me her favour for all that I had done [in propitiating the lady] of the turquoise every day. Amount of the offerings of every day: bit-bread ---- ----- 350, white bread 320, beer 360, wine 30, ro-geese 60 ------- water 100, for I went down to the coast successfully. None other peer of mine equalled me of any who had come to this [foreign country], I being the favourite of Hathor, <lady of> the turquoise.'" [33]

See below for another depiction from a similar relief which is notably showing the MFKZT or what can be described as white powder gold in figure 16:

Figure 16

Once again it appears as though an offering is being given in a bowl to the mouth area. This looks like it is to be eaten. This can be assumed since you can see on the other side of the depiction the offering to the mouth area is some sort of drink out of a tea pot. Here is a narrative of the scene:

This stele had the following entry in "The Inscriptions of Sinai":

In the lunette are the winged disk and uraei with the cartouche and titles of the king, 'The good god, lord of the two lands Nebmare, endowed with life eternally'. The lunette is closed at the bottom by the symbol of heaven, below which is a double scene, showing, on the left, the king, 'Son of Re Amenhotep, ruler of Weset', offering a conical loaf on a cup to 'Sopdu, the great god of the east', and, on the right, the king, 'The good god Nebmare', offering two small vases of water to Hathor. The inscription, 'Beloved of Hathor, lady of the turquoise', at the same time refers to the king and also gives the name of the goddess, a double reference common in these scenes. Both deities are standing on a common pedestal and are therefore meant to be statues. In the central column we read, 'Said by Hathor, lady of the turquoise: "(I) am giving thee millions ----"'.

Below is an inscription of twenty-three lines which, as far as is legible, reads as follows: 'Year 36, second month of winter, day 9, under the majesty of the king of Upper and Lower Egypt, Nebmare, son of Re, Amenhotep, ruler of Weset, endowed with life like Re eternally and for ever. Behold his majesty was in the southern city (= Thebes) - - - - - - - - - of Weset. Behold it was entrusted to the king's scribe, overseer of the Treasury [Sebek]hotep called Pinhasy to make ------ turquoise, while his majesty was celebrating the third sed-festival - - - - - - - - - - - - on the last day of the month ------ from Hathor, lady of the turquoise (?) in joy, while her heart was glad, [she] rejoicing [in what] Nebmare [had done for her] - - - - - - - - - jubilating and laughing (?) ------- Pinhasy (?) - - - - - - - - - - who had come forth with him were joyful. The leaders were glad of heart and his work waxed mightily, each one treading this hill country adoring (?) this goddess, their scribe who was, in their midst giving praise daily, Amenmose whose name is Memay (?) ------- being present (?). This scribe says: I followed my lord in the hill country; I took hold on the task which he had entrusted to me; I went forth on the ocean to foretell the wonders of Punt, to obtain the odorous gums; I brought away the foreign princes in their --- (?) --- with the tribute of numberless hill countries. Behold I have come also and trod the country of this goddess; I directed work for turquoise, I received - - - - - - L.P.H. He gave the gold of reward, the mouths rejoiced - - - all - - - -, all commands, work-people ---- I found --- sea --- in his reaching the [southern] city - - - '

It is not clear what the "gold of reward" is or who is giving it but it is interesting to note that the thing being given in the picture is the "conical loaf in a cup". Whether this "white bread" is the same as the white ORMUS [or mono-atomic gold] materials is open to question. The inclusion of the white bread shape in the gold inventory at Karnak is very suggestive but it is not definitive. 33

Although it might not be blatantly obvious, on its own accord, what the "gold" conical reward was, once this has been compiled together with the rest of the overwhelming evidence surrounding this strange white powdery substance one begins to see a web of circumstance. In a court of law sometimes without direct evidence pointing towards proof a strategy of creating circumstantial evidence is attempted. That is what we are seeing here. There is a building heap of circumstantial evidence around this mystery powder. In fact, it was even found scattered within one of the unearthed Egyptian temples, "Sir Williams Flinders Petrie unearthed a temple on the Sinai Peninsula, at Mt Serabit, near Serabit El Khadim in 1903 which was full of alchemical iconography from the time of the 3rd Egyptian Dynasty. In this temple complex was found literally tons of white powder composed of monatomic platinum group elements. An alchemical crucible was also unearthed." [34]

Thutmose III, who also can be argued as being the same as Moses who we would identify in the bible, has been seen in reliefs as being instrumental in creating a group of people who regularly consumed monoatomic gold. These reliefs tell an eerily occultist story in the Temple of Karnak:

It was, in fact, Pharaoh Tuthmosis III who had reorganized the ancient mystery schools of Thoth and founded the Royal School of the Master Craftsmen at Karnak. They were called the Great White Brotherhood because of their preoccupation with a mysterious white powder. A branch of this fraternity became especially concerned with medicines and healing, to become known as the Egyptian Therapeutate. Then, in much later times, the activities of the Therapeutate were extended into Palestine - especially into the Judah settlement of Qumrân, where they flourished as the Essenes.

But, what was so special about the goddess Hathor that she was the chosen deity of the Sinai priests? Hathor was a paramount nursing goddess and, as the daughter of Ra, she was said to have given birth to the sun. She was the originally defined Queen of the West and Mistress of the Netherworld, to where she was said to carry those who knew the right spells. She was the revered goddess of love, tombs and song - and it was from the milk of Hathor that the pharaohs were said to gain their divinity, becoming gods in their own right.

On one of the rock tablets near to the Mount Serâbît cave entrance is a representation of Tuthmosis IV in the presence of Hathor. Before him are two offering-stands topped with lotus flowers, and behind him is a man bearing a conical cake identified as white bread. Another relief details the mason Ankhib offering two conical bread-cakes of shem-an-na to the king, and there are similar portrayals elsewhere in the temple complex. One of the most significant perhaps is a depiction of Hathor and Pharaoh Amenhotep III. The goddess holds a necklace in one hand, while offering the emblem of life and dominion to the pharaoh with the other. Behind her is the treasurer Sobekhotep, who holds in readiness a conical cake of white bread. Most importantly in this portrayal, however, is the fact that Treasurer Sobekhotep is described as the 'Overseer of the secrets of the House of Gold, who brought the noble and precious stone to his majesty'. [35]

Here are some photos of Karnak reliefs showing some interesting Thumose III and IV scenes with the conical white powder cakes. This relief is called the *Annals of Thumose III at Karnak*. It shows the spoils that he collected from his military campaigns, which there were many. Look to the right side of the picture, and you will see many bowls with the conical cakes of white powder placed in them. He is counting them as part of his spoils from a confrenation in the Syria region. This would have been considered the area where Nannar-Sin (Enlil) from the Annunaki would have hailed. [36] See figure 17:

Figure 17

So as the reader may be surmising by now, many of the ancient texts have a common theme of collection of this wondrous powder of gold. You find it in the Sumerian tablets, the Torah, the Bible's Old Testament and in ancient Egyptian reliefs. But is there another popular text in which this unusual compound might be found? How about the New Testament? Do we find it there? Does Jesus have anything in common with this white powdered gold?

In short, the answer is, yes. Not only does it circumstantially surround his activities, but he also talks about it in his parables on many occasions. Here is a section, defined within a sermon by Jack Harris, in the Book of

John, where he describes a parable and a detailed description of Manna. This fact is clearly evident in the dialogue between the Jews of Jesus' day and the Lord Himself. "So they asked Him, 'What miraculous sign then will you give that we may see it and believe you? What will you do? Our fathers ate the manna in the desert; as it is written: "He gave them bread from Heaven to eat." Jesus said to them, I tell you the truth, 'it was not Moses who has given you the bread from Heaven, but it is my Father who gives you the True Bread from Heaven. For the Bread of God is He who comes down from Heaven and gives life to the world .'" [37]

As you read the passages below you will notice that Jesus, since he always speaks in multi-level parables, might also be talking about the consumption of manna in addition to the traditional explanation. We are taught that as long as we eat of his flesh and drink his blood, meaning eat of his ways and believe in him, then we will surely ascend to heaven. But what if he also means that we have some help? What if manna can also help us become better people, better neighbors, and more loving, understanding human beings? This must be worth valuable consideration. In the Book of John 6:31-56 is where Harris discussed the following excerpts:. In its entirety it becomes more apparent as to what Jesus truly meant, of course, on another allegorical level:

31 Our ancestors ate the manna in the wilderness; as it is written: 'He gave them bread from heaven to eat.'[a] "

32 Jesus said to them, "Very truly I tell you, it is not Moses who has given you the bread from heaven, but it is my Father who gives you the true bread from heaven.

33 For the bread of God is the bread that comes down from heaven and gives life to the world."

34 "Sir," they said, "always give us this bread."

35 Then Jesus declared, "I am the bread of life. Whoever comes to me will never go hungry, and whoever believes in me will never be thirsty.

36 But as I told you, you have seen me and still you do not believe.

37 All those the Father gives me will come to me, and whoever comes to me I will never drive away.

38 For I have come down from heaven not to do my will but to do the will of him who sent me.

39 And this is the will of him who sent me, that I shall lose none of all those he has given me, but raise them up at the last day.

40 For my Father's will is that everyone who looks to the Son and believes in him shall have eternal life, and I will raise them up at the last day."

41 At this the Jews there began to grumble about him because he said, "I am the bread that came down from heaven."

42 They said, "Is this not Jesus, the son of Joseph, whose father and mother we know? How can he now say, 'I came down from heaven'?"

43 "Stop grumbling among yourselves," Jesus answered.

44 "No one can come to me unless the Father who sent me draws them, and I will raise them up at the last day.

45 It is written in the Prophets: 'They will all be taught by God.'[b] Everyone who has heard the Father and learned from him comes to me.

46 No one has seen the Father except the one who is from God; only he has seen the Father.

47 Very truly I tell you, the one who believes has eternal life.

48 I am the bread of life.

49 Your ancestors ate the manna in the wilderness, yet they died.

50 But here is the bread that comes down from heaven, which anyone may eat and not die.

51 I am the living bread that came down from heaven. Whoever eats this bread will live forever. This bread is my flesh, which I will give for the life of the world."

52 Then the Jews began to argue sharply among themselves, "How can this man give us his flesh to eat?"

53 Jesus said to them, "Very truly I tell you, unless you eat the flesh of the Son of Man and drink his blood, you have no life in you.

54 Whoever eats my flesh and drinks my blood has eternal life, and I will raise them up at the last day.

55 For my flesh is real food and my blood is real drink.

56 Whoever eats my flesh and drinks my blood remains in me, and I in them. [38]

Some of this not only makes the reader wonder if he is talking about Enki or Anu as his father, but also if the Annunaki are the keepers of this manna; or at least whether or not they are the keepers of the knowledge of creating manna. Maybe it's both, since Enlil represents destruction and

Enki represents creation and protection, as well as manna is identified as a gift from the Heavenly Father. So if we are to consider that manna is a gift from the heavens, then maybe we were given the gift within our DNA that as long as we seek Christ, Manna, then we can increase the importance of the Christ-like characteristics within ourselves. Are we moving into an age where we are allowed to openly participate in the evolution of self-awareness and develop a Christ-like consciousness? Is this the coded message Jesus Christ is trying to share to those who seek understanding? It is becoming apparent that through the collective Christ consciousness, we are being gifted permission to pursue both a 'collecting' of divine cosmic manna, as well as gaining access to the knowledge of this jump-starting substance known as mono-atomic gold. Either way we choose to pursue, it is ultimately up to each individual to walk this path. Jesus only gives us the *hope*, which gives us the confidence that it is actually possible for us all!

# 7 MODERN USAGE OF MONO-ATOMIC GOLD

Although this can be quite a subjective topic, since the idea of a multi-dimensional substance is brand new from a modern perspective, it is not so subjective to those who have been making it and experimenting with it for decades. The people learning about this substance actually range from self-proclaimed Alchemists to large scale agriculture firms and gold mining giants. I will shine light and show respect for all members here. I believe there is no doubt that this subject and substance needs the attention of the world so we can not only understand who we are and where we came from, but also so we can understand where we are headed.

What is Mono-Atomic Gold or any other Mono-Atomic element for that matter?

Classical science teaches us that the three phases of matter are gasses, liquids, and solids (and the newer plasmas, Bose-Einstein condensates and liquid crystals). Some solids crystallize into a lattice structure called metals. What classical science does not teach us is that there is, in fact, another phase of matter called monatomic. These monatomic materials have ceramic-like properties.

Microclusters - Nuclear physicists discovered in 1989 that the atoms of some elements exist in microclusters. These are tiny groups of between two and several hundred atoms. Most of the transition group precious metals in the center of the periodic chart exhibit a monoatomic state. If you have more than a specific number of these atoms in a microcluster, the atoms will aggregate into a lattice structure with metallic properties. If you have fewer than that critical number of atoms, that microcluster will disaggregate into monatomic atoms with ceramic properties. Monatomic atoms are not held in position by electron sharing with their neighboring atoms as are atoms in a classical lattice structure. The critical number of atoms for rhodium is 9 and the critical number of atoms for gold is 2...

It has been observed that the valence electrons of monatomic elements are unavailable for chemical reactions. This means that monatomic atoms are chemically inert and have many of the physical properties of ceramic materials. Because the valence electrons are unavailable, it is impossible to use standard analytical chemistry techniques to identify a monatomic element.

What the observer says may be true but he doesn't explain the physical mechanism at work here. Are the valence electrons unavailable for reactions in monatomic elements or not? Also, simply assigning a name to a phenomena doesn't explain the phenomena.

These are very recent discoveries and the full implications have yet to be evaluated by the scientific community. You won't find this in textbooks yet.

In general, a metallic element is physically stable and is a relatively good conductor of both heat and electricity and is usually chemically active. (Metals typically rust and/or corrode.) To the contrary, monatomic atoms of the same element behaves more like a ceramic in that they are generally poor conductors of both heat and electricity and are chemically inert. In addition, according to Hudson, monatomic elements exhibit the characteristics of superconductors at room temperature.

Russian scientists at the Institute of Mineralogy, Geochemistry, and Crystal Chemistry of Rare Earth's in Kiev explicitly state in their literature that atoms in lattice structures are metallic in nature and that these same atoms in the monatomic state are ceramic in nature. However, Dr. Kogan of the institute does not support all of Hudson's findings as being scientifically valid. It would be worthwhile if we could obtain a detailed critique of Hudson's work from that institute.

Monatomic atoms have been observed to exist in all the heavy elements in the center of the periodic table. These are the elements which have "half-filled" bands of valence electrons and include the following elements. Their atomic numbers are given in parenthesis (the atomic number represents the number of protons in the nucleus.) Ruthenium (44), Rhodium (45), Palladium (46), Silver (47), Osmium (76), Iridium (77), Platinum (78), and Gold (79). Other metallic elements in the same part of the periodic table have also been observed in microclusters. Because the atoms of monatomic elements are not held in a rigid lattice network, their physical characteristics are quite different from atoms which are locked in the lattice. Thus, it is the grouping of atoms which defines the physical characteristics of the element; not just the number of neutrons and protons in the nucleus as previously believed. If you don't have a lattice network, you don't have a metal even though the atoms of the two forms of matter are identical!

The implication here is that there is an entirely new phase of matter lurking about the universe. This form (phase) of matter is comprised of monatomic elements; a heretofore unknown form (phase) of matter. They have remained unknown for so long because they are inert and undetectable by normal analytical techniques.

This might be nothing but a scientific curiosity except for the fact that Hudson now claims that a relatively large amount of this previously undiscovered monatomic matter seems to exist in the earth's crust.

Limitations of Analytical Chemistry - How could it be that a small percentage of the earth's matter could be comprised of material which heretofore has been completely undiscovered? It has to do with the theory of analytical chemistry. None of the detection techniques of analytical chemistry can detect monatomic elements. They can only detect elements by interacting with their valence electrons. Because the valence electrons of monatomic atoms are unavailable, the atoms are unidentifiable. To detect a monatomic element requires that you first convert it from its monatomic state to its normal state to allow the element to be detected with conventional instrumentation. As a result, this phase of matter has existed as a stealth material right under the noses of scientists without detection until very recently.

Some observers claim that there should be reliable detection techniques for monatomic matter but you have to know what you are looking for to make use of the techniques. If you do not suspect that monatomic matter exists, it is unlikely you will accidentally find it.

Peculiarities of Monatomic Elements - The monatomic form of an element exhibits physical characteristics which are entirely different from its metallic form. These differences are currently being investigated by nuclear physicists so it isn't possible to make an exhaustive list of the differences. A few of the differences will be noted.

Classical literature states that the white powder has a fluorescent-like glow. [David] Hudson says that this powder behaves as a superconductor at room temperature, giving it very interesting properties. Because it is a superconductor, it tends to "ride" on the magnetic field of the earth, giving it the powers of levitation. It has been found to be very difficult to determine the specific gravity of monatomic elements because the weight varies widely with temperature and the magnetic environment. Under some circumstances, monatomic elements weigh less than zero! That is, a container full of monatomic matter could be observed to weigh less than the empty container.

Noble metals produce an extreme concentration of 'superfood'. The conductivity which feeds the building blocks of life and higher consciousness. These are high quality monoatomic elements.

These are also known as ORMES (Orbitally Rearranged Monoatomic Elements) or ORMUS and m-state elements, and the newest theories in physics as they relate to this area of research assert that some elements on the periodic chart might be diatomic (two atoms) or small atomic cluster "condensates," which are known in the scientific community as "Bose-Einstein Condensates." [39]

As you can see, much will be discovered once modern chemistry catches up to the amateur chemists who have been researching this extraordinary substance for quite some time. The only caution I would add, since this will be discussed in the last chapter, is that there is a reason this substance is not being identified in mainstream science. If it can be suppressed it will. I can only hope that at least by introducing the idea of the Mono-Atomic production plant (which we previously called a pharoah's tomb), we can begin to ask the right questions. I want the truth, and this is where it is leading me, so I believe we must exhaust it to the end. On that note, who is David Hudson, as the above article so adeptly eluded to, as the modern discoverer of these Orbitally Rearranged Mono-atomic Elements?

Hudson was a farmer and miner in the Phoenix, Arizona area and had some issues with his soil, which caused him to perform some drastic acts in order to correct the soil to allow for growth. With regard to his farming, he states that his soil was too alkaline and water would not penetrate the soil to allow seed to sprout. He would water and water it and then soil would repel the water as if it were completely water proof. This caused him to look into applying acid to his soil so he could loosen it up for water penetration. When he cannibalized his sulfuric acid from the mining venture, he used it as his acid to flip the pH of his soil and maybe get it back to neutral - eventually. The first contact he made with the ORMEs was most likely at this point because he spoke about seeing a foaming action erupt; then after the reaction died down, he noticed an unusual white substance caked on the top of the soil. He had it analyzed and it came back as "undefined inert ingredients" several times. This peaked his interest, and then began to experiment with this process in his metal mining venture.

This is the point his world turned upside down, and he stumbled down a rabbit hole. We get to watch this tumbling unfold in his Dallas presentation. The following presentation is a set of transcripts from a Dallas, TX conference where he told his most unusual story of what happened next. [Please note, this is a somewhat lengthy excerpt, but Hudson is the only credible person right now who actually has come up with conclusions regarding Mono-Atomic Elements, so it is all critical in comprehending what this mystery substance truly is. I wanted to make sure you had a chance to see it.]:

Basically this is the story of my quest for this material [Mono-Atomic Gold and ORMEs]. To get an understanding of it, to be able to explain what it is. And my work began in this area for all the wrong reasons. I did not understand what I was doing. And I don't need it. Ah, I didn't understand what the material was and it's only in the last four or five years that I've really come to an understanding, understanding truly of what the material really is. But basically the work began about 1975-76, and my primary interest for getting into this area is, was, like I say, for all the wrong reasons.

I am from Phoenix, Arizona. My father is the ex-commissioner of agriculture in the state of Arizona. My mother is the, was the state Republican's woman chairman. We're ultra-ultra right-wing conservative. Very, very ultra conservative people. All of my farming was done on a handshake basis. I even farmed 2,500 acres on a handshake with the Bureau of Indian Affairs and that's the federal government and no one farms with the federal government on a handshake and a verbal agreement but I did...

...Anyway, I began buying gold and silver in the Phoenix area as bullion from refiners. Most of it was being refined from sterling silver scrap or electronic scrap. But, ah, a lot of the gold was coming from miners who were processing it by a process called "heap leach cyanide recovery". And they were heap leaching, um, these old tailings on these mining operations. I became very intrigued with this because we were very interested, in agriculture, in metal salts in our soils. I don't know, I think that here in Dallas it's much the same or further on west in the state, it's much the same as Arizona. We have a sodium problem in our soil. It's called "black alkali" and as the black alkali builds up in your soil you can put sulfuric acid on the soil and the sodium, which makes up the black alkali, becomes sodium sulfate, which is a white alkali. And then is water soluble and will leach out of your soil then. If you don't do this your soil is very oily and the water just won't penetrate and be retained by the soil and it's not very good for your crops.

And so we had been doing soils analysis and this concept of, of literally piling ore up on a piece of plastic and spraying it with a cyanide solution, which dissolves selectively the gold out of the ore. It trickles down through the ore until it hits the plastic and then runs out the plastic and into the settling pond. It's pumped up through activated charcoal where the gold adheres to the charcoal and then the solution is returned back to the stack. And the concept seemed pretty simple, and I decided, you know, a lot of farmers have airplanes, a lot of farmers have race horses, a lot farmers have race cars... I decided I was going to have a gold mine. And, I had earth movers and water trucks and road graders and backhoes and caterpillars and these kind of things on the farm and I had equipment operators, and so I decided I was going to set up one of these heap leach cyanide systems.

I traveled all over the state of Arizona, took about a year and a half, and I finally settled on a piece of property. And, ah, did some analysis and all and decided that this was the property that had the gold in it that I wanted to recover. I set up a heap leach cyanide system, began spraying the ore, and sure enough within a matter of a couple days, we hooked it up to the activated charcoal. And we analyzed the solution going in the charcoal. We analyzed the solution coming out of the charcoal and we were loading gold on the charcoal. And, you know, everything is just rosy. We're having a high old time. And I figured I could lose 50 percent per year mining gold and be as well off as buying the gold and paying taxes at 50 percent on the, on the profit with buying the gold. So, if other people had to mine gold and make a living, I could mine gold and lose 50 percent, and be as well off as making the money, paying income tax and buying gold with it. So I figured, hey, I ought to be able to do that.

So, what happened is, ah, we began recovering the gold and silver and we would take the charcoal down to our farm. We'd strip it with hot cyanide and sodium hydroxide. We'd run it through "electro winning cell". We'd get the gold out on the "electro winning cell". And then we would do what's called a "fire assay" where you run it through a crucible reduction, cupelling, and get this gold and silver dore' bead. Now I am not going to elaborate on all this because I am not trying to teach anybody "fire assaying". I am just trying to explain the procedures here. This is the time honored procedure for recovering gold and silver and basically , it's, it's been performed for 250-300 years. It's the accepted standard in the industry.

[11:24] Ah, after we recovered this gold and silver for a couple of weeks, we began to recover something else. And the something else was recovering as if it's gold and silver but it wasn't gold and silver. Our beads of gold and silver were actually getting to the point that you could hit them with a hammer and they would shatter. Now there's no alloy of gold and silver that will become that brittle. Gold and silver are both very soft metals and they don't alloy in any proportion that would cause them to become hard or brittle. Yet this became very hard and brittle. When we sent it to the standard laboratories for analysis, all they could detect was gold and silver with traces, and just traces, of copper. Something was recovering with the gold and silver. We couldn't explain. And eventually it got so much of this in our recovery system that actually we were losing gold and silver when we recovered this other material. And so, you know, it wasn't supposed to be profitable, it's just supposed to be something that was interesting.

And so I said, "Shut the system down. You know, let's find out what the problem material really is". And chemically we were able to separate the "problem material" from the gold and silver and I had this sample of pure problem stuff, whatever it was. And you have to understand my background is cotton farming. I did take pre-law, decided to go into agriculture but I hated chemistry, I hated physics, like most of you. And ah, I decided, well heck, you know if you just pay enough money to the right experts, you can hire enough Ph.D's, you'll be able to figure this problem out. So I went to Cornell University, where a man had written these papers on doing x-ray analysis and he took the sample of the problem material, which wouldn't dissolve in any acids or bases, as separated. It was cobalt blue in color. And he did an analysis on it and he told me it was iron silica and aluminum. I said it's not iron silica and aluminum. He said, "Well sorry that's what the analysis says it is". So, working within Cornell, we removed all of the iron, all the silica and all the aluminum from the sample. We still had over 98 percent of the sample. At this point he said, "Dave, it analyzes to be nothing". (audience laughter)

He said, "Mr. Hudson, if you'll give us a $350,000 grant, we'll put graduate students to working on it". Well I had paid him about $12,000 thus far. He told me he could analyze anything down to parts per billion and now he's telling me I had pure nothing. He didn't offer to refund any of my money and so I said, "No thank you, I think for $350,000 I can get more information than you can". That was about 1981 and basically I embarked on a research program of my own. Most of the information that directed me initially was just hearsay. The old time miners, the people who's dads had mined in Arizona, who's grandfather's had mined said, "Dave, what you're working with is the platinum group elements". There's been hundreds of people who believe the platinum group elements are there. Many of them are incarcerated in jail right now. Ah, they go out, they believe the elements are there, and so they go to investors and they say, you know, "We think they're there, so put this money in", and the people put the money in. A couple years later they don't have any salable commercial product and so the investment collapses and the investor sues them. And eventually they are convicted or exonerated but it always ends up in bitter feelings.

[15:30] And so I said, you know, "I am not going to allow this to happen with this project. I'm going to fund the thing myself and I am going to get the answers to it". I mean this is 1981-82. We had instrumentation and machines that will analyze down to parts per billion. You know, this has to have some explanation to it. Ah, the man at Cornell, he could show me the atoms, he could tell me how far apart they were, but he said the emission and absorption spectra does not agree with any spectra that we have programmed into our machine... but it didn't give me any of the answers.

So, I was handed a book called 'The Analytical Chemistry of the Platinum Group Elements' by Ginzburg. It was written in 1975. It was translated into English by the Israeli Program For Scientific Translation. And this book, it's probably about 2 1/2 inches thick, it's a hard bound technical book, put out by the Soviet Academy of Sciences. Now when you realize that Johnson Matthey and Englehard are the two miners and refiners of the Platinum group elements in South Africa. The other miners and refiners are the Russian government. The Russians basically got into this after 1918 when they threw, the, Johnson Matthey, out of their country, because they were, the British were married to their royal family, and they had a deal going where royalties were being paid to them for the mining of their platinum group elements. And so, the Russian government in 1918 committed to develop this separation chemistry for these elements.

Basically these elements were not all that important until about world war two and then they became very strategically important. Right now they're classified as strategic elements and any important government contracts that are issued, they're classified under strategic classification. So you don't use them unless you absolutely have to because they are so valuable and so rare. They use them like.... iridium is used on the nose-cone of the re-entry vehicle on the space shuttle. It's used on the hydrogen rocket shields that deflect the heat shield on the hydrogen because it's a very high temperature ceramic. It's used in the breaker circuitry on the nuclear power plants where they have to disconnect the power, reconnect it, and they need something that can stand tremendous arcs and not deteriorate. You know, these kinds of uses where nothing else will work.

And so basically, what happened is, according to the Soviet Academy of Sciences, they said that to analyze for these elements by emission spectroscopy, you'd have to do a procedure called fractional vaporization where you literally put the powders to be analyzed on the carbon electrode and you burn it for 300 seconds...

...And sure enough, exactly in the sequence, and exactly as the Soviet Academy of Sciences said, these elements began to read. They came off in the sequence, exactly in the order and exactly as they were supposed to come off. There's palladium, platinum, ruthenium, rhodium, iridium and osmium. And at the time I didn't even know what iridium was. I didn't know what rhodium was...

[22:39] Okay, it's a material that nothing else will do what it does. The only thing is, the numbers we were reading, and we did these studies for 2 1/2 years, the numbers were 4-6 ounces per ton of palladium, 12-13 ounces per ton of platinum, 150 ounces per ton of osmium, 250 ounces per ton of ruthenium, I mean, yeah, ruthenium, 800 ounces per ton of iridium, and 1,200 ounces per ton of rhodium. Now when you understand that the best known deposit in the world, to date, is approximately 1/3 of one ounce per ton in South Africa, and they have to go 1/2 mile underground to mine a 30 inch seam that contains this 1/3 of one ounce of all the platinum group elements. And we have over 2,400 ounces per ton of platinum group elements. Now if this had just been 5 or 6 ounces per ton I probably would have laid it down and walked away from it. But because the numbers were so preposterous, so ridiculous, so unbelievable, I said, you know, "Let's go for it. Let's find out what really is going on".

We're talking about 12-14 percent of this rock was these elements. I said, you know, "This, this has to have an explanation. There has to be a reason why nobody's ever found this material. Nobody's ever understood it."

So I went to a Ph.D. analytical chemist in Phoenix who was supposedly the best that Arizona had. He was a Ph.D. analytical chemist, a graduate of Iowa State University, with a specialty in metal separation systems. He had worked for Sperry and Motorola and all these electronic firms doing waste water treatment. I told him the story about the spectroscopy work that we did for these three years and he said, "You know Mr. Hudson, I've heard the story about the platinum group elements all of my life. I'm a native Arizonan also." But he said, "All I have to sell is my reputation and this makes me very nervous because of the frauds and the promotions and all". And he said, "Tell you what I'll do, I'll work for you at no charge. I won't charge you like everybody else has, until I can tell you where you're wrong. And at that point I'll submit you a bill at $60 an hour for my time." He said, "If I bill you up front I have to issue reports and if I issue a report I have to sign my name, and I'm not comfortable signing my name until I totally understand this".

[25:25] Two years later this Ph.D. said, "Dave, I can, without equivalence, I can tell you that it is not any of the other elements on the Periodic Table." He said, "I have physically separated, in the past, every element on that Periodic Table. All the rare earths, many of the Actinides, the man-made elements. He said, "I've done them all. I've worked with niobium, strontium, niobium, titanium, all the electronics materials." He said, "I've done all these studies for all these companies, but there are four elements that I have never worked with, and that's four of the six that you brought me...

...Now the Ph.D. says, "Dave, in all my years working with Pacific Spectrachem, I have never had any problems with these people. Never. Until I met you." And he said, "What we have here is something that I know is pure rhodium and yet none of these spectroscopic analyzes are saying it's rhodium." Iron could be a reddish brown chloride, but silica and aluminum and calcium do not form colored salts at all. And yet if you take the material that they claim is silica and calcium and re-dissolve it through a fusion and hydrochloric acid, and you got the red brown chloride again. Now where did it come from? And he says, "Dave, this makes absolutely no sense at all. This is defying everything I have been taught in college, everything I have been taught in graduate school". So, what he did, he said, "I'm going to send this back to my graduate professors at Iowa State." So we took these red brown chloride solutions in hydrochloric acid. We evaporated down the salts and they were these blood red chloride salts, okay, and we sent these to Iowa State University and we said, "What is the metal that's present in this salt?"

And Iowa State University came back, "There's chlorine present". Well, chlorine's a gas. Well, fine, there's chlorine, but what is the chlorine reacting with that makes it a crystalline material? And they said, "There's chlorine present". And we said, "Yes, but what's the metal that holding the chlorine?" They couldn't tell us.

...I probably got the best credentials money can buy. I got a man that worked, now, a total of 9 1/2 years, he's a Ph.D. analytical chemist, he physically can separate and quantify everything known to man. And he says, "Dave I can't explain this. This is not explainable."

So we finally ordered from Johnson Matthey, pure standard materials of rhodium and iridium, platinum, palladium, ruthenium and osmium and we learn how to make them disappear. We could take pure rhodium chloride and analyze it to be pure rhodium, and through a process of repeated evaporation with salt, we could make the rhodium disappear from the instrumental analyzes. It still is a blood red chloride, you still can perform all the chemistry, it still was in solution but it didn't analyze to contain any rhodium. And this was pure rhodium standard.

The way it disappeared was a process of disaggregation. So when we became comfortable that, you know, I don't [know] what this is or what form it is, but I know what it is. We actually took pure standards of metal, put them in our separation system and they separated right where they were supposed to be, as these elements.

When I went back and talked to them [at General Electric], I met with about 7 people back there, and they turned me over to their senior catalytic chemist, his name was Tony LaConti. He said, "Dave, we know that when we buy the commercial standards from Johnson Matthey that they analyze very well, but we do know that when we convert through a fusion process to disaggregate them to a finer particle size, that they do not analyze as well as they used to." So, his suggestion to me was, "Dave, I don't care whether it analyzes or not. Your credentials behind you are as good as we have anyplace at GE. Just send us the material and we'll mount it in our fuel cells and if it does what it's supposed to do, who cares what you call it"...

And so at the time our material is ready to work with, the people weren't at GE anymore, they were at Waltham, Massachusetts, so we contracted with these people to do the fuel cell testing.

Our material as delivered to Giner analyzed and contained, the rhodium didn't contain any rhodium, the iridium didn't contain any iridium. But when it was mounted on carbon and put into a fuel cell, it did what only rhodium would do. It was a hydrogen evolving catalyst and it was carbon monoxide stable. Okay? It does what only, at that time, about $10,000 an ounce rhodium would do. Now I understand rhodium is down probably a thousand an ounce now. But it did what only rhodium would do. We ran the fuel cells for about three weeks doing time studies on it, and at the end of the three weeks they tore down the fuel cells and sent the carbon off for analyzes, and now we have 6 percent rhodium on the electrodes. Mysteriously appeared from some place, 6 percent.

[36:47] They said, "Dave, to our knowledge no one knows that rhodium can exist in this state. No one knows that iridium can exist in this state. In fact, if you want, you can patent this. If you can explain it, if you can tell how to make it from a known commercial material, you can put a patent on this." So I went to their patent attorney in Washington, D.C., and in 1988 I filed U.S. and worldwide patents on 11 elements in their orbitally rearranged monatomic state. Okay? That's where the name comes from, and we just made it up on an airplane one day. Orbitally Rearranged Monatomic Element. We knew that the chemistry changed. We knew that the material became totally inert and did not act like a metal. We knew that it did not have any valence electrons available for chemical bonding, and we knew that there was a change in the nuclear configuration. We didn't understand it yet but we knew it was the case.

And so, this material was, went to the U.S. patent

office. In addition we filed another 11 patents on another phenomena. And this phenomena becomes very interesting. If you take a gram of gold and you convert it, through a disaggregation process to the monatomic form, the last product you have before it goes to pure mono atomic material, is hydrogen auride or hydrogen rhodide or hydrogen iridide. Which if you know this is a minus one state. Coincidentally. Hydrogen is more electropositive than these elements. So it's not gold hydride, it's hydrogen auride. Which is in the literature if you are curious. Anyway, when we anneal away the proton, the material goes snow white. All of these elements in their pure mono atomic form are snow white. They look just like cooking flour. [WOW!!!] You know, you ladies who do cooking, just look for that white bleached flour that you pour out in a little measuring cup. Doesn't look like a metal at all. The hydrogen auride is gray, but the pure dehydrogenated material is snow white. It is very fluffy. It has a density of about 2 1/2 yet the metal has a density of about 19. Okay?

This is not at all like it's supposed to be, but it's there and it's these elements. The amazing thing about it is the weight of the material was very difficult to weigh. We were having all this crazy weights on it, so in trying to quantify this on paper for the patent office, and they want things very precise at the patent office, we couldn't get consistent results with the material. It kept gaining weight and gaining weight and gaining weight and gaining weight and gaining weight, you know, and so what's the correct weight, you know?

So we got a machine called thermo-gravimetric analysis. ...you put metals in there and oxidize them and see the weight gain of the oxide and hydrogen reduce, and see the loss of the oxide. Or you can heat it up to high temperatures and when it thermally decomposes, you can tell that the weight's going because the weight's coming down on the scale...

...when the material goes snow white, it weighs 56 percent of the true weight. Now that should bother you, I hope. You say, where's the mass going? Why isn't it weigh-able anymore? And by repeated annealing we could make the material weigh less than the pan weighed it was sitting in, which was less than nothing, or we could make it weigh 300-400 times what it's beginning weight was, depending on whether we were heating or cooling it. Yet the machine is built with magnetic standards, that you could actually put in the machine, and the materials are non-magnetic, then at a certain temperature they become magnetic, then at another temperature they lose their magnetism, to check the machine and see if there's any effect of it's magnetic field from the heating coil that's effecting the weight of the material. And yet the magnetic materials have no effect at all. Yet when you put this material in and literally take it quantitatively to the white form, the material only weighs 56 percent of the true weight.

Yet if you take this white powder and put it on a quartz boat, and heat it up to the point where it fuses with the quartz, it becomes black and it regains all it's weight again. This makes no sense, it's impossible, it can't happen. But there it was.

So, we became interested in the area of why this material was changing it's weight. We went to Varian Corporation [Varian Associates Inc., 3050 Hansen Way, Palo Alto, CA, 94304 (415) 493-4000] over in Stanford, we showed them the data, and they said, "Mr. Hudson, if you were cooling a sample, we would say it's a superconductor"...

[44:40] You've seen in these science magazines where they've got a picture of the brain and they show part of the brain lit up when you eat something sour or you see another part light up when you eat something sweet or that's electric seizure where the brain just lights up all over. How do they see these thought patterns in your brain? With superconductors. Superconductors can sense any disturbance in a magnetic field. They're unbelievably sensitive. And, so if this material is a superconductor, even this tiny little bit of magnetic field that was still around the heating coil, the material could levitate or it could sink, because a superconductor will not break lines of magnetic force when they're superconducting. They resist moving in the field and so they would tend to levitate or they couldn't be weighed. If you pick the scale up they're gonna weigh more, or if you put the scale down they're gonna weigh less, because they're not moving. So if it's a superconductor this is not really a good thing to be doing. It doesn't really mean anything.

When I began to do the literature studies, I found out that in a macro-metal, the temperature of the atoms is actually being measured now over in Europe. And the temperature is about 350 degrees Kelvin, depending on the metal, I mean, more or less. About 350 degrees. As you disaggregate the clusters in that metal down smaller and smaller, the temperature of the atom goes down and down. A three atom cluster is about 23 degrees Kelvin, a two atom cluster is about 12 degrees Kelvin, and a 1 atom, they don't know what it really is because they can't read it, they can't find it. But theoretically it's about 2 to 3 degrees Kelvin. The internal temperature inside a single atom is, in fact, almost absolute zero. It has nothing to do with temperature of the room it's sitting in, and actually what we were doing is, we were heating and cooling a monatomic system, and the monatomic system was giving up energy. And so we set up to do differential thermal analyzes and we found out there was a lot more heat coming out than we were putting in when we heated it.

We have that chart too in graph. Then actually by heating it, we were cooling the atoms, because the temperature had nothing to do with the internal temperature of the atom. The only way it could hold energy is through chemical binding or through crystalline binding and there was none of that going on because it 's a monatomic system. We actually found that these atoms, in the literature, since we filed our patent, and we filed 11 more patents on the superconducting state of a mini-atom system of the high-spin state. We found in the published literature in 1989, 1990 and 1991, that the Niels Bohr Institute, that Argon National Laboratories, that Oak Ridge National Laboratories, indeed had confirmed that the very elements that I had filed in my patents do exist in this high-spin state, in the mono atomic form. And that they do inherently go to that state when they're in the mono atomic form. They will not go to this state when they're in the diatomic state, but they will go to this state in the mono atomic form. And the words that they have developed in the scientific community to explain this is the asymmetrical deformed high-spin nuclei. They have even published papers on the asymmetrically deformed high-spin nuclei, and found that they theoretically should be superconductors. Because high-spin atoms can pass energy from one high-spin atom to the next with no net loss of energy. Okay?...

...and in the asymmetrically deformed high-spin state, and they are stable in that state, and they are not radioactive isotopes in that state. But it is a state that will only occur in the monatomic form. When they are in this state they do not want to go back to metal. They repulse each other. They will not go to a metallic state until you get the spin state back to the low spin state.

The Philosopher Stone was a white powder of gold. The Philosopher Stone was said to be the container of the light of life.

We took some calves brains and some pigs brains, and we did a destruction of the organic material and a metals analysis and over 5 percent, by dry matter weight, of the calves brains and the pigs brains, were rhodium and iridium in the high-spin state. And nobody in medical research knows that.

I found in the literature, and I'll show you those tomorrow, the U.S. Naval Research Facility has confirmed superconductivity is the communication vehicle between cells in our body, but they don't know where the superconductivity comes from. It's like it's a stealth atom that no one can figure out what it is. (audience laughter) It's there but no one can read it, just like this stuff.

When you realize that the Philosopher Stone is the white powder of gold, then, of course, I have to find out does it work? Does it really have the properties they attribute to it? Which they claim that not only it will cure every disease known to man, they claim that it is capable of changing the nature of man, making him into a different person.

(audience break - lecture then continues)

Okay, back to the alchemical substance. When I became interested in this alchemy, because the white powder of gold was the alchemical substance supposedly, I began to do all sorts of reading, and one of the things I came across immediately was the Melchizedek priesthood and the white powder of gold associated with the Melchizedek priesthood. So I went to Rabbi Plotkin at Temple Beth Israel in Phoenix, and I asked the Rabbi, who is one of the most knowledgeable rabbis in Arizona, I said, "Rabbi, have you ever heard of the white powder of gold?", and he said, "Oh yes Mr. Hudson, but to our knowledge no one's known how to make it since the destruction of the first temple". He said, "The white powder of gold is the magic. It can be used for white magic or black magic".

And when you really find out what the white powder of gold is, you begin to really appreciate that statement. So, anyway, as I began to research this further, I found out about the history of it, I found out that it has been associated with the ancient peoples over in the Tigris-Euphrates valley. It was knowledge that was given to them by, they claimed, the gods. It is always depicted in the literature as a triangular shaped stone, but it's about twice as tall as it is wide, kind of an elongated pyramidal shape, like this. I think Zecharia Sitchin refers to it as the "athinder? stone". Ah, but all of their sacred text always began with it. Curious enough, in the ancient Egyptian text it was always referred to as the "What is it?", and if you read in the papyrus of Ani that was found in the tomb of Pepe the 2nd in old kingdom Egypt, it says, "I am purified of all imperfections, what is it, I ascend like the golden hawk of Horus, what is it, I come by the immortals without dying, what is it, I come before my father's throne, what is it, and it goes on and on, page after page, talking about all these attributes that you acquire as you ascend, but they always stop and ask the question, "What is it"?

Well, this was written about 28-29 hundred B.C., and they're asking this question "What is it"? Well when I found the Hebrew dictionary, I found out that the Hebrew word for "What is it?" is Ma-Na. Manna literally means the same thing, "What is it?" And when you understand that the Hebrew people were actually, lived in Egypt for generations, they were the artisans, they were the metallurgists, they were the craftsman. And when they left out of Egypt they took this knowledge with them. We find in the literature that, and this is particularly in Velikovsky's writing, 'Ages in Chaos', that he says, that, eh, when the Egyptian..., when the Hebrew people left Egypt that the Egyptians decided that they wanted to go after them and they find the writings in Egypt where the Pharaoh and his army drown in a whirlpool of water.

Now this right at the end of old kingdom Egypt.

Remember in the Bible, that it says that the Hebrews encountered these mean, warring like peoples called the Amalekites out on the Sinai peninsula as they were exiting Egypt, and they, Moses wanted to fight them, and the Hebrew people said "naw, these guys are fierce tribesmen, there's hundreds of thousands of them, we don't want to fight these people". And so they avoided fighting them. Well, Velikovsky found out that at the very same time they were having all the plagues in Egypt they were also having plagues over in the Tigris-Euphrates valley, and the ruling tribe, the Amalekites, exited the Tigris-Euphrates valley at the same time the Hebrews were exiting Egypt. And they literally passed each other on the Sinai with the Amalekites coming west as the Hebrews were going east. They arrived in Egypt and there was no Pharaoh and there was no army, and literally, these Arabs, destroyed and killed everyone. All they left were the lesser people, who they kept as slaves for themselves, but they hacked and killed and slaughtered everyone. They destroyed the temples, they wiped out a very high culture at the end of old kingdom Egypt. By the time they woke up to the fact of what they had destroyed, the knowledge that was gone, it was too late. The only people that knew how to make it, who were still alive, were the Hebrews, and they were out on the Sinai.

They began in ancient Egypt to do the opening of the mouth ceremonies, they begin to mummify their leaders, waiting for this knowledge to come back so that the leaders could be brought back to life, but in fact the knowledge was gone. And so, if you look in old kingdom Egypt, did you know that they've never found the body of a pharaoh or a high priest from old kingdom Egypt? Never. And they claim in their literature that they never died, that they ascended the stairway to heaven. And when you read about what they did and where they went, it totally agrees, they were going to the very same place that the people in the Tigris-Euphrates valley went to, to ascend the stairway to heaven. And that was to an island called Bahrain, it's just off the Sinai peninsula. There was a city by the name of 'Kilmun' or 'Dilmun' and do you know that they have excavated the city and found that it does exist, and it's supposedly the land of the crossing, where the fresh water and the sea water mix. And they have found the fault, right underneath the island where fresh water exits under the ocean and mixes with the sea water.

All of this goes back to writings about the first mortal king in the Tigris-Euphrates valley, Gilgamesh, and his quest for immortality. It goes back to he was told to travel to the land where the sun rises, which in fact was the name for Arabia. And he traveled down the Tigris-Euphrates river, and into the ocean and across the ocean, they came to this island, and it was at that island where the man who survived the flood lived, and that's the man we know as Noah, that he was looking for. The man who lived 900-1,000 years, and has three sons who lived over 900 years, who had this knowledge.

Okay, now we come back to the Hebrews who exited Egypt. All of the Egyptians that had this knowledge were slaughtered, and no one was there to bring them back to life. But the Hebrews had this knowledge, and Bezaleel, the goldsmith, was commanded by Moses to prepare the "What is it?", the manna, or the "bread of the presence of God", which was another name, they knew it in old kingdom Egypt. In old kingdom Egypt they had three other names for it, it was called "the golden tear from the eye of Horus", it was called "that which issues from the mouth of the Creator", the spittle, or it was called "the semen of the Father in Heaven". And if you take the white powder gold and you mix it with water, it forms a gelatinous white suspension, that, as a farmer I can attest, it does look just like semen, which we use to, for the cattle and all. Ah, that would be a good description of it, if I was trying to convey to someone what it looks like.

Basically this is the basis of all religions of the world. How many times have you heard "cleanse yourself", "purify yourself", "prepare yourself like a bride in the bridal chamber", "for the coming of the father". What they don't go on and tell you is what happens in the bridal chamber, you become inseminated in the bridal chamber. But you receive the semen of the father in Heaven. And you. . . over. . . this is done over a 40 day period during a 40 day fast. It was called the Egyptian rite of passage. It went 9 days with no food to totally cleanse the digestive system, and they took this material, or the "semen of the Father in Heaven", for the next 30 days. Okay, it was called "the Bread of Life" and the "Bread of Life" was mixed with the water and was called the "Living Water". Okay? This material is what Moses commanded Bezaleel, the goldsmith. It wasn't a baker, it wasn't a woman, it was a goldsmith who was told to prepare the "Bread of the presence of God", and this "Bread of the presence of God" was set out on a golden table in front of the Ark of the covenant. You remember the ark of the covenant, they also placed the stones, through which God spoke to Moses, and gave him the ten commandments.

And the Bible says, up on Mt. Sinai, that the Hebrew people said there was fire and there was smoke. It was if a forge was going up on Mt. Sinai. But when you recall that Moses had been there previously and in the area of Sinai is where copper was being mined and smelted. And in fact, I believe there was a forge going on Mt. Sinai, because at 1,160 degrees the white powder of gold can be melted to a transparent glass of gold. It literally becomes a glass as clear as window glass, and yet it is pure gold, it's not a gold compound, it's pure gold. You can take it in a mortar and pestle and grind it right back to the white powder, but it is, it looks absolutely like glass.

The neat thing about gold, as compared to the other elements, is that gold can be purified by distillation. At 450 degrees elemental gold will resonance disconnect from itself and will go over as a gas and be re-condensed over here and be caught as white powder again. And so you can purify it, back and forth, by repeated distillation, and get a very high purity substance. It's called the "white dew", the "white condensate", "the white dove" or it's depicted as a white feather in the alchemical texts. Because that's the way it was purified as a volatile material. Okay? All of the symbols of being fed by a dove, or receiving the white dove, is always an alchemical symbol. When we find, as the rabbi told me, that this knowledge was kept by the Hebrews until the destruction of the first temple.

What happened when they destroyed the first temple? And what happened right before the temple was destroyed? We find that Solomon got a woman pregnant who came from Egypt and she, in fact, was the Pharaoh of Egypt. What was her name, Hatshepsut? How do you pronounce it? Hatshepsut? Anyway, it was in fact the Pharaoh of Egypt that came to Solomon's temple, and she became pregnant, she returned back to Egypt, and she gave birth to a son, and the son's name was Menelik. Menelik returned to Jerusalem when he was twenty one to be acknowledged by Solomon as being his son. And Solomon, of course, acknowledged Menelik, "Yes, you are my son". And of course, the Levites, the high priests, just went bonkers. Here was a half breed. And they had all this racial purity, and here was a half breed as the eldest son of Solomon, to be the next king of Jerusalem. And so the Levites said, "You must send your son away, he must be sent away". And Solomon, in his infinite wisdom, said, "Fine, if I must send my son away, all of you Levites must send your eldest sons away also". So all of the eldest sons of the Levites left with Menelik, but when they left they took the Ark of the Covenant.

And that's where the Ark of the Covenant went; to Egypt. When the Hebrews realized that the Ark of the Covenant had left, these men who took it were the ones who by blood right were the correct ones to care for it. They were the eldest sons of the Levites and the king. But because they were sent away they took the Ark of the Covenant. And the Hebrew people haven't really wanted to talk about this that much, because it really was their doings that they lost it. And so, the Aaronic priesthood or the rabbinical priesthood does not want to talk about the high priesthood leaving Jerusalem, but it went to Egypt. And it was kept in Egypt out on the island of Elephantine, where they built an exact duplicate of the Temple of Solomon, and you'll read, and find out about that, if you read Graham Hancock's book, 'The Sign and the Seal'. This is all in there and it is absolutely correct. They have excavated. The excavators have found, on the island of Elephantine, the exact dimensions of the Temple of Solomon, where the foundation was and where the Ark of the Covenant was kept. In the temple of Luxor they recorded all of the loot and all of the plunder that was taken from the Temple of Solomon by Thutmose II, was then returned when he became pharaoh and looted the temple. But there's no Ark of the Covenant because they already had that. And in that plunder they list all of the items that they got, and they're all identified as being golden, and then silver and then copper. But under the golden items, under the shewbread, here is this elongated pyramidal shape that is "The Bread of the presence of God". It's the very same symbol, that I told you earlier, that is always shown as depicted in the sacred ceremony, with the king offering the "bread", the "white bread", to the symbol of the Ark of the Covenant, with the black Anubis sitting on top of it. Well the Anubis represented the digestive system, and here's the king offering, and it says "keeper of the secret", but it's the white powder of gold being offered to the digestive system, which is the transformational process you go through.

Now, what does it do? I'm not a doctor so I can't practice medicine. Anything that is administered to someone for the purpose of curing a disease is medicine. So therefore I can't tell you on tape what's been done with it, what the doctors who have giving it have done with it, but I can tell you that at 2 mg. it totally has gotten rid of Karposi Sarcomas on AIDS patients, at 2 mg. per day. 2 mg. per day. There's 32,000 milligrams in an ounce, 2 mg. is nothing. And it gets rid of "KS". I can tell you that people who have taken it, at 2 mg. injections, within 2 hours, their white blood cell count goes from 2,500 to 6,500 white blood cells. I can tell you that stage 4 cancer patients have taken it orally, and after 45 days have no cancer anyplace in the body. We're not gonna go into any more specifics than that. I will talk to you about it later when the cameras aren't running.

I am not a doctor. My purpose in this was not to cure diseases and illness, but I did want to know "does it work"? It's been used on Lou Gehrig's disease, it's been used on MS, it's been used on MD, it's been used on arthritis, it's been used on, ah, what else, that's all that's coming to mind right now, and it just does some very remarkable things in the body. The most important thing that it does and the real reason this is here is not as a medicine.

The reason this material is here is to enlighten and raise the consciousness of mankind. Now if people don't understand that, I apologize, but that really is its purpose. And what we have done is we have given it in the high amounts to some people who have had nothing wrong with them medically. We didn't know what to expect. So the very first man, he did a 42 day food fast, which is pretty severe food fast. He went for 9 days with only water, he had a high colonic, and on the 10th day we began to give him 500 mg a day of this material. Now this was not gold. This was rhodium and iridium. And the reason we chose rhodium and iridium is because it naturally was in his body. It's in Aloe Vera gel. It's in Ace Mannan. It's in "Man aloe". It's in carrot juice, it's in grape juice, it's in grape seed extract, it's in slippery elm bark, it's in sheep sorrel, it's in many, many materials. And so it's totally natural, it's not a compound, it's not a drug. It's an elemental material. It's like taking an iron pill. But these are the atoms that flow the light of life in your body.

And according to ancient Egyptians, they said, "You have a physical body, you have to feed physical foods to so it can grow and become all that it's meant to be. If you don't feed your material body, you die or you're very stunted. You don't grow and develop." You also have a light body, they said, you also must feed so it can grow and become what it's meant to be. And we haven't been feeding our light body, because we haven't known what to feed it with.

500 mg. a day for 30 days, was called the Egyptian rite of passage, and so we had to find out what does this do. After 5 or 6 days of taking this material, this fellow began to hear this very high frequency sound, and every day the sound gets louder, and louder, and louder, and louder, and louder and louder. By the time he finished his fast, he said it's like loudspeakers in my brain, literally roaring this sound. It's the same sound that many of the meditators have heard, that you're told to listen for when you meditate, to find this sound, but when you think about it most people don't hear it anymore. Well this sound is roaring in this man's head, it's roaring day and night, it's roaring when he's talking on the phone, it's roaring when he's working. And I said, "Doesn't this disturb you? Isn't this an irritating sound? " and he said, "Not at all. It's just like nectar", because it doesn't come through the ears. He said, "It's inside the brain."

Now it's hard for me to understand. It's hard for probably most of you to understand. He says, "David, it's just nectar. It's something that you literally want to go within the sound and just let it exclude everything out of your life". Basically at the end of the 42 day fast, he went back, he took a body brush to get rid of the toxins in his body, and he went back eating normally. And he was eating meat, white meat and vegetables. Well he figured the sound would die down and go away. It doesn't. The sound is still growing and getting louder and louder. After 60 more days, the dreams begin, the revelations begin, and then the visions begin. And this is going to sound a little far fetched to some of you, but there are light beings that come to this man and teach him. They never open their mouth but they telepathically are communicating with him. And with the hope that I'm not going to offend anyone, there actually is a female being that comes to him and has sex with him.

And I didn't understand this until I found in the ancient Vedic texts that it talks about this, having sex with the angels. 2000 B.C. After about 7 months, he begins to have orgasms. And this is an adult group basically so I better explain to you, he has no erection, he has no seminal emission, but it's an orgasm. I say, "Is it nice?" and he said, "It's just like the real thing". He's now having about 7-8 a day.

He said, "Dave, the sound seems to originate about 8 inches above my head, it comes down into my brain, it's like a hat band around my head, and it just roars here in my head. I can feel the vibration all through my body". But after 7 months these orgasms started and they just got more frequent and more frequent, and it's not something he controls. It's something that just comes on. Well, he only sleeps about an hour and a half to two hours now, he doesn't need 7-8 hours like most of us, and so he decided one morning about 4 o'clock in the morning, he's gonna go outside and just let this orgasm go. See what happens. He said it began down the pelvis, and it literally, he just let it move, and he said he could feel it, it came up over his stomach, up over his chest, up over his head, and he said, "My whole body was involved in this orgasm". And he said, "I felt hot. I felt like if someone came up and touched me they would burn their hand. Then all of a sudden, out of the top of my head, goes this column of energy". He feels it just going right out the top of his head.

Ah, I was, about three weeks ago, I was handed a book, called "Secrets of the Golden Flower" by Richard Wilhelm with an introduction by Carl Jung. Richard Wilhelm did the eastern translations for Jung. This book was written in 1931, and it's been translated and been reproduced, and published several times since then, I guess it's now in paperback because some people are getting paperback copies now. Anyway, it verbatim describes this sound. And it says in the book it seems to all be about this sound, the "hu". Well we are the hu-man. The man who can hear the sound. Okay? This is about the "hu", the sound. And that it says in there that you get this energy in your pelvis, and that it can be developed where it literally will take your whole body up over your head and everything. And when it finally is at a state of perfection that it will feel like there is a column of light coming right out the top of your head.

I think the word that most people use for it is the kundalini. But that's what it is. This man can cut cards now, and hold them up, and tell you what the suit is and what the number is, and he's right 10 out of 10 times. He can tell you who's going to come to see him tomorrow, he knows what they're going to want to talk about before they get there, who it's going to be, what they are going to want to talk about. He says there's this complete feeling of oneness with all living things, all animals, all humans. It's just this total unity of oneness with all life.

According to the "Secrets of the Golden Flower", it takes 10 lunar months, which happens to be the same as the Egyptian's said, 9 solar months, same time frame, but at the end of this, at the ninth month, he literally becomes a light being. It's the breaking through of the cosmic egg, and he literally becomes a light being, capable of levitating and capable of bio-locating. To literally disappear here and reappear someplace else.

Now this sounds pretty preposterous, except if he's a perfect superconductor, he can levitate, he can walk on water. And tomorrow I will share with you some of the papers by Harold Puthoff, down in Austin, Texas, who worked on the government contracts on psychic, telepathy, mental connections between people, and he's now working with levitation, time travel and all that. He's published some papers developing Sakharov's theory about gravity, in which he says, that gravity is not a gravitational field. That gravity, is in fact, the inter-reaction of matter, the protons, and the neutrons and the electrons, with the zero point, or vacuum energy. And what we experience as gravity is, in fact, the inter-reaction of the matter with the zero point energy. That there is no gravitational field per se. And in his calculations and in his mathematics, he calculates that when matter is resonance connected in two dimensions, it no longer interacts in three dimensions, but it's only interacting in two dimensions, by what he calls the jitterbug motion, that it loses 4/9s of it's gravitational weight. Or it only weighs 56 percent, which if you all recall is exactly what our material weighed. 56 percent, or 5/9s of it's true weight. Which means that the material is a resonance connected, quantum oscillator, resonating in two dimensions, which just happens to be the definition of superconductor.

But when I met Hal Puthoff, he said, "Dave, you know what this means, it means, when you can control space-time, if you control gravity, and you control gravity, you are controlling space-time. And so literally what these atoms are doing is they are bending space-time to weigh 5/9s. He says, "There are theories in the published journals, credible journals, about moving faster than the speed of light, from one place to another. But to do it you must have what's called exotic matter, matter that has no gravitational attraction at all." Do you know that iridium at 70 degrees Fahrenheit, has no gravitational attraction at all, and that 70 degrees Fahrenheit is the temperature of your body, or above, or that your body's above that. And so literally if our body becomes filled with the light, we literally eat this until our light body exceeding our physical body, then we supposedly become light beings.

And our physical body no longer controls our light body, our light body now controls our physical body. And anywhere we can think we would like to go, we can travel there not only spiritually, but physically, and take our physical body with us. Now coincidentally, in the Bible, this is referred to as the rapture. It says, two will be working in the field and one will be gone, two will be laying in bed and one will be gone. It will be a physical taking up and disappearing from where you're at. It says in Revelations, 'Blessed be the man who will overcome for he shall be given the hidden manna, the white stone of purest kind, up on which will be written a new name." [Rev. 2:17] You will not be the same person you were before you took the material. It actually says you will have a new name,

you will be a different person. When you become filled
with the spirit, when you become filled with the chrism,
you are not the same person you were before. All of that
DNA that these biomedical people can't figure out what
it's it in your body for, it's actually there to function, it just
isn't working right now.

Right now we only use 8-10 percent of our brain.
What's the other 90 percent there for? Did we evolve a
brain that we don't use? I don't think so. It's like at some
ancient time we used that brain, and we used that DNA,
and we were a different person. Well that sure sounds
awfully philosophical, doesn't it. The Bible says that at one
time we were the Adam Kadmon, we were the angelic
being, and we have fallen to this animalistic state. But in
the Bible, it says, that the day will come when the ancient
of days returns here to Earth. Who is the ancient of days?
The ancient of days is the Adam Kadmon, the original
man and when this man returns here and he literally can
read your thoughts in your mind without you opening your
mouth, how much more could you ever be judged? No
more skeletons in the closet, no more hidden agendas.
Everything's known. In the Bible they call it the opening
of the book of life.

It's the time that everything gets judged, everything gets
revealed. And then, and only then, will you see Christ
again. That's when he returns. Okay? In Revelations, it
says, the streets of the new Jerusalem, will be paved with
gold so pure as like unto transparent glass. [Rev. 21:21]
Gold so pure as like unto transparent glass, and the
foundations are made of gold like unto transparent glass.
[Rev. 21:18]

Now if that isn't heavy enough for you, when I found
out that the name for the golden tree of life was the
ORME, ormus or ormes. And the name of my patent is
Orbitally Rearranged Monatomic Elements. In the Book
of Isaiah, it says a latter day David, a descendant of the
Davidic blood line, my cousin, bless her soul joined the
Mormon Church, and they had her do her genealogy, and
my great-great-great grandmother, was Hanna de Guise,
daughter of Christopher de Guise, brother of Charles or
Claude de Guise, who if you got a copy of "Holy Blood
Holy Grail" there, Charles or Claude de Guise is in the
book. Nostradamus worked for the de Guise family and

Nostradamus prophesied by 1999 the occult gold will be known to science. Very specific prophecy, very exact dates, very precise. And a descendent of this family, a latter day David, is the one who's to plant the Golden Tree of Life.

And I didn't know any of this when I filed my patent. And so when you realize what this is, and you realize what it does, and you realize why it's here, then you realize why my job is not to make money with it. I can't make money with it. My job is to tell those people who are ready for it what the state of things are and when it's going to be available. I can't sell it, I will solicit donations to cover our costs in producing it. But it has to be made available for those people who are ready for it.

And this is called the Lesser Keys of Solomon, the Keys to the Kingdom. Remember the Petra, the Rock, held the keys to the Kingdom, Peter, the Keeper of the Keys? And this is called the Keys to the Kingdom. It's not the answer, but it's the door that unlocks, it's the key that unlocks the door to the answer. You no longer have to die to literally come face to face with the angels, to experience what most of these people call, when they died and came back to life, it's an unbelievable feeling of oneness. The closest most of you will ever be to another person is during the moment of sex. Think about it? And yet this is even more than that. Because you're one heart and one mind with everyone. Somebody said it would make a great title for a book, "Better Than Sex".

Well, it is all about love, total oneness with everyone. It's perfect telepathy, perfect communication, it's total love and total oneness. When you understand that superconductors don't have to touch, okay, we're back to the science again. In electricity, the wires have to touch before electricity can flow from one wire to another wire, but superconductors can sit at a distance, and as long as they are in resonant harmony, and their Meissner fields touch, they are one. Because they flow light between them. So they act as one superconductor. So when you are a perfect superconductor, and she is a perfect superconductor, you are one with her heart and her mind. You know all things about her. Perfect telepathy. And that is the Judgment. That is the Oneness.

Now what does it do in the body? It literally corrects

the DNA, by a process the equivalent of a denaturing solution, the DNA relaxes and recombines corrected. So all diseases that originate with a problem with the DNA can be corrected, but your reason for taking it cannot be to correct a disease. Your reason for taking it has to be a philosophical reason. It has to be to enlighten and to raise the nature of mankind. If in doing that, it happens to cure the diseases, so be it...

When you no longer need to eat, when you literally can be fed on the resonance fields of the universe. All you need is water. When you no longer need energy, you can travel anywhere you want just by thinking where you'd like to be and be there. When you can live 800-1,000 years with perfect body, literally every cell in your body perfected and corrected. And then your metabolism speeds up about 45 or 50 percent, you return to the state you were when you were a teenager and you can stay in that state.

This is what the material is.

We don't have all the answers yet. There's a tremendous amount of research study that needs to be done by the medical people on it. We have an awful lot of doctors already working on it. AIDS, cancer all working on it. We have National Institute of Health licensing and permitting to do it. And, ah, all I can tell you is it's here, it ain't going to go away if you don't believe it, and ,ah, it will change the world more than anything in the last 2,000 years. [40]

So we learned that this mono-atomic element group can become superconducting material at certain temperatures, become static in its existence and perform in its environment without the equivalent of weight as we would understand it. It can communicate by resonating and disregards the law by which the speed of light resides. It can help humans regenerate and return to a super healthy state, in which some cases is better than some test subjects ever experienced. Needless to say it appears this monoatomic substance gives us the ability to potentially live in more than one dimension, as we currently understand dimensions. But mentioning that this presentation that Hudson gave was in the mid 1990's, it would be important to note any additional studies regarding monoatomic gold and health could add to our knowledge.

The only one which can be found to date, which would coincide with this theory, would be the "Realm of Aging." Anti-aging is an industry in and of itself. Everyone who enjoys life wishes they could live longer, if not forever, especially if this could be achieved in a young-looking and young-feeling, healthy state!

# 8 MONO-ATOMIC GOLD AND TELOMERES

The aging process is in the back of everyone's mind almost all the time, especially for those over a certain age. For most I would venture to say it becomes a foremost thought by the age of 25. From there, it's all downhill as they say. Or is it? Are Mono-Atomic Elements the key to stopping or even reversing this inevitable process of age-related deterioration? It might just be.

Recently, it was discovered that as chromosomes divide they retain a healthy end cap "device" that retains all the genetic material within the chromosome. If this end cap degrades and disappears, the genetic material escapes and thus the cell encapsulating the chromosome dies. So what is this "end cap"? What is it made of? It is called the telomere. Here is a high magnitude microscopic photo of chromosomes with telomeres. The red portion is the chromosome and the genetic material within and the yellow or gold (aptly colored I must say) material on the ends are telomeres.

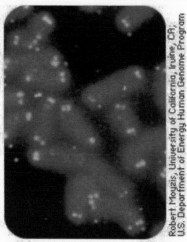

Robert Moyzis, University of California, Irvine, CA;
U.S. Department of Energy Human Genome Program

It's so beautiful.    It almost looks like pixie dust scattered around, guarding the life within doesn't it?  Here is an article from the University of Utah defining the telomeres titled, *"Are Telomeres the Key to Aging and Cancer?"*

Inside the center or nucleus of a cell, our genes are located on twisted, double-stranded molecules of DNA called chromosomes. At the ends of the chromosomes are stretches of DNA called telomeres, which protect our genetic data, make it possible for cells to divide, and hold some secrets to how we age and get cancer.

Telomeres have been compared with the plastic tips on shoelaces because they prevent chromosome ends from fraying and sticking to each other, which would scramble an organism's genetic information to cause cancer, other diseases or death.

Yet, each time a cell divides, the telomeres get shorter. When they get too short, the cell no longer can divide and becomes inactive or "senescent" or dies. This process is associated with aging, cancer and a higher risk of death. So telomeres also have been compared with a bomb fuse.

What are telomeres?:

Like the rest of a chromosome and its genes, telomeres are sequences of DNA - chains of chemical code. Like other DNA, they are made of four nucleic acid bases: G for guanine, A for adenine, T for thymine and C for cytosine.

Telomeres are made of repeating sequences of TTAGGG on one strand of DNA bound to AATCCC on the other strand. Thus, one section of telomere is a "repeat" made of six "base pairs."

Telomere Length:

In human blood cells, the length of telomeres ranges from 8,000 base pairs at birth to 3,000 base pairs as people age and as low as 1,500 in elderly people. (An entire chromosome has about 150 million base pairs.) Each time a cell divides, an average person loses 30 to 200 base pairs from the ends of that cell's telomeres.

Cells normally can divide only about 50 to 70 times, with telomeres getting progressively shorter until the cells become senescent, die or sustain genetic damage that can cause cancer.

Telomeres do not shorten with age in tissues such as heart muscle in which cells do not continually divide.

Why do chromosomes have telomeres?:

Without telomeres, the main part of the chromosome - the part containing genes essential for life - would get shorter each time a cell divides. So telomeres allow cells to divide without losing genes. Cell division is needed so we can grow new skin, blood, bone and other cells when needed.

Without telomeres, chromosome ends could fuse together and degrade the cell's genetic blueprint, making the cell malfunction, become cancerous or die. Because broken DNA is dangerous, a cell has the ability to sense and repair chromosome damage. Without telomeres, the ends of chromosomes would look like broken DNA, and the cell would try to fix something that wasn't broken. That also would make them stop dividing and eventually die.

Why do telomeres get shorter each time a cell divides?:

Before a cell can divide, the chromosomes within it are duplicated so that each of the two new cells contains identical genetic material. A chromosome's two strands of

DNA must unwind and separate. An enzyme (DNA polymerase) then starts to make two new strands of DNA to match each of the two unwound strands. It does this with the help of short pieces of RNA. When each new matching strand is completed, it is a bit shorter than the original strand because of the room needed at the end by this small piece of RNA. It is like someone who paints himself into a corner and cannot paint the corner.

Does anything counteract telomere shortening?:

An enzyme named telomerase adds bases to the ends of telomeres. In young cells, telomerase keeps telomeres from wearing down too much. But as cells divide repeatedly, there is not enough telomerase, so the telomeres grow shorter and the cells age.

Telomerase remains active in sperm and eggs, which are passed from one generation to the next. If reproductive cells did not have telomerase to maintain the length of their telomeres, any organism with such cells soon would go extinct.

What role do telomeres play in cancer?:

As a cell begins to become cancerous, it divides more often, and its telomeres become very short. If its telomeres get too short, the cell may die. It can escape this fate by becoming a cancer cell and activating an enzyme called telomerase, which prevents the telomeres from getting even shorter.

Studies have found shortened telomeres in many cancers, including pancreatic, bone, prostate, bladder, lung, kidney, and head and neck.

Measuring telomerase may be a new way to detect cancer. If scientists can learn how to stop telomerase, they might be able to fight cancer by making cancer cells age and die. In one experiment, researchers blocked telomerase activity in human breast and prostate cancer cells growing in the laboratory, prompting the tumor cells to die. But there are risks. Blocking telomerase could impair fertility, wound healing, and production of blood cells and immune system cells.

What about telomeres and aging?:

Geneticist Richard Cawthon and colleagues at the University of Utah found shorter telomeres are associated with shorter lives. Among people older than 60, those with shorter telomeres were three times more likely to die from heart disease and eight times more likely to die from infectious disease.

Dr. Richard Cawthon Dr. Richard Cawthon:

While telomere shortening has been linked to the aging process, it is not yet known whether shorter telomeres are just a sign of aging - like gray hair - or actually contribute to aging.

If telomerase makes cancer cells immortal, could it prevent normal cells from aging? Could we extend lifespan by preserving or restoring the length of telomeres with telomerase? If so, does that raise a risk the telomerase also will cause cancer?

Scientists are not yet sure. But they have been able to use telomerase to make human cells keep dividing far beyond their normal limit in laboratory experiments, and the cells do not become cancerous.

If telomerase could be used routinely to "immortalize" human cells, it would be theoretically possible to mass produce any human cell for transplantation, including insulin-producing cells to cure diabetes patients, muscle cells for muscular dystrophy, cartilage cells for people with certain kinds of arthritis, and skin cells for people with severe burns and wounds. Efforts to test new drugs and gene therapies also would be helped by an unlimited supply of normal human cells grown in the laboratory.

How big a role do telomeres play in aging?:

Some long-lived species like humans have telomeres that are much shorter than species like mice, which live only a few years. Nobody yet knows why. But it's evidence that telomeres alone do not dictate lifespan.

Cawthon's study found that when people are divided into two groups based on telomere lengths, the half with longer telomeres lives five years longer than those with shorter telomeres. That suggests lifespan could be increased five years by increasing the length of telomeres in people with shorter ones.

Once a person is older than 60, their risk of death doubles every eight years
People with longer telomeres still experience telomere shortening as they age. How many years might be added to our lifespan by completely stopping telomere shortening? Cawthon believes 10 years and perhaps 30 years.

Once a person is older than 60, their risk of death doubles with every eight years of age. So a 68-year-old has twice the chance of dying within a year compared with a 60-year-old. Cawthon's study found that differences in telomere length accounted for only 4 percent of that difference. And while intuition tells us older people have a higher risk of death, only another 6 percent is due purely to chronological age. When telomere length, chronological age and gender are combined (women live longer than men), those factors account for 37 percent of the variation in the risk of dying over age 60. So what causes the other 63 percent?

Some factors in aging:

A major cause of aging is "oxidative stress." It is the damage to DNA, proteins and lipids (fatty substances) caused by oxidants, which are highly reactive substances containing oxygen. These oxidants are produced normally when we breathe, and also result from inflammation, infection and consumption of alcohol and cigarettes. In one study, scientists exposed worms to two substances that neutralize oxidants, and the worms' lifespan increased an average 44 percent.

Another factor in aging is "glycation." It happens when glucose sugar from what we eat binds to some of our DNA, proteins and lipids, leaving them unable to do their jobs. The problem becomes worse as we get older, causing body tissues to malfunction, resulting in disease and death. This may explain why studies in various laboratory animals indicate that restricting calorie intake extends lifespan.

It is possible oxidative stress, glycation, telomere shortening and chronological age - along with various genes - all work together to cause aging. [41]

So if we were to battle aging, or just to prevent the process from accelerating, it would behoove us to know how to protect these telomeres. This was touched on briefly in the University of Utah article, but of course this deserves much more respect and attention. They mentioned Telomerase as the enzyme which helps to rebuild and repair the telomeres. It sounds as if the telomerase enzyme is the maintenance chemical or "worker" that is in charge of its health. Telomerase obviously deserves some elaboration doesn't it?

In an article titled, "'Fountain of Youth - Telomerase: Scientists Successfully Map Enzyme That Has Rejuvenating Effect On Cells" written in the Science Daily, they go into detail as to what role this enzyme plays in rebuilding the telomeres:

> The mapping of telomerase may boost our knowledge of cancers and their treatment, says Stig E. Bojesen.
>
> Mapping the cellular fountain of youth -- telomerase. This is one of the results of a major research project involving more than 1,000 researchers worldwide, four years of hard work, DKK 55 million from the EU and blood samples from more than 200,000 people. This is the largest collaboration project ever to be conducted within cancer genetics.
>
> Stig E. Bojesen, a researcher at the Faculty of Health and Medicial Sciences, University of Copenhagen, and staff specialist at the Department of Clinical Biochemistry, Copenhagen University Hospital, Herlev, has headed the efforts to map telomerase -- an enzyme capable of creating new ends on cellular chromosomes, the so-called telomeres. In other words, a kind of cellular fountain of youth.
>
> "We have discovered that differences in the telomeric gene are associated both with the risk of various cancers and with the length of the telomeres. The surprising finding was that the variants that caused the diseases were not the same as the ones which changed the length of the telomeres. This suggests that telomerase plays a far more complex role than previously assumed," says Stig E. Bojesen.
>
> The mapping of telomerase is an important discovery, because telomerase is one of the very basic enzymes in cell biology. It relengthens the telomeres so that they get the same length as before embarking on cell division.

"The mapping of telomerase may, among other things, boost our knowledge of cancers and their treatment, and with the new findings the genetic correlation between cancer and telomere length has been thoroughly illustrated for the first time," says Stig E. Bojesen.

The human body consists of 50,000,000,000,000 or fifty trillion cells, and each cell has 46 chromosomes which are the structures in the nucleus containing our hereditary material, the DNA. The ends of all chromosomes are protected by so-called telomeres. The telomeres serve to protect the chromosomes in much the same way as the plastic sheath on the end of a shoelace. But each time a cell divides, the telomeres become a little bit shorter and eventually end up being too short to protect the chromosomes. Popularly speaking, each cell has a multi-ride ticket, and each time the cell divides, the telomeres (the chromosome ends) will use up one ride. Once there are no more rides left, the cell will not divide any more, and will, so to speak, retire. But some special cells in the body can activate telomerase, which again can elongate the telomeres.

Sex cells, or other stem cells which must be able to divide more than normal cells, have this feature. Unfortunately, cancer cells have discovered the trick, and it is known that they also produce telomerase and thus keep themselves artificially young. The telomerase gene therefore plays an important role in cancer biology, and it is precisely by identifying cancer genes that the researchers imagine that you can improve the identification rate and the treatment.

"A gene is like a country. As you map it, you can see what is going on in the various cities. One of the cities in what could be called Telomerase Land determines whether you develop breast cancer or ovarian cancer, while other parts of the gene determine the length of the telomeres. Mapping telomerase is therefore an important step towards being able to predict the risk of developing different cancers. In summary, our findings are very surprising and point in many directions. But as is the case with all good research, our work provides many answers but leaves even more questions," says Stig E. Bojesen. [42]

Although highlighting the importance of this enzyme, this study did not actually breakdown its makeup. All it did was identify that it was important and played a significant role in aging of normal cells, as well as cancer cells. But what is it really made of? Because if you can find the right "food" for the correct type of telomerase, which repairs the telomeres of the normal cells, then you in-turn have isolated your best chance at endless, healthy cell division for eternity. This assumes you can find it and consume it. So, without further au due, ladies and gentlemen behold the study which has identified the food for the "Holy Grail" enzyme, telomerase. This is the elixir of life; the fountain of youth. The following abstract identifies a study which proved that nanoparticles of Gold (AuNPs), or in our language within this book, MONO-ATOMIC GOLD:

Although the telomeric repeat amplification protocol (TRAP) has served as a powerful assay for detecting telomerase activity, its use has been significantly limited when performed directly in complex, interferant-laced samples. In this work, we report a modification of the TRAP assay that allows the detection of high-fidelity amplification of telomerase products directly from concentrated cell lysates. Briefly, we covalently attached 12 nm gold nanoparticles (AuNPs) to the telomere strand (TS) primer, which is used as a substrate for telomerase elongation. These TS-modified AuNPs significantly reduce polymerase chain reaction (PCR) artifacts (such as primer dimers) and improve the yield of amplified telomerase products relative to the traditional TRAP assay when amplification is performed in concentrated cell lysates. Specifically, because the TS-modified AuNPs eliminate most of the primer-dimer artifacts normally visible at the same position as the shortest amplified telomerase PCR product apparent on agarose gels, the AuNP-modified TRAP assay exhibits excellent sensitivity. Consequently, we observed a 10-fold increase in sensitivity for cancer cells diluted 1000-fold with somatic cells. It thus appears that the use of AuNP-modified primers significantly improves the sensitivity and specificity of the traditional TRAP assay and may be an effective method by which PCR can be performed directly in concentrated cell lysates.
43

This Abstract was developed by a group of graduate students at UC Santa Barbara and may not fully understand the relevance, that is until they read this book, how significant this discovery was. They literally applied mono-atomic gold to the telomerase and it strengthened and lengthened! This is truly amazing. This is significant evidence that moves towards proving beyond a reasonable doubt that Mono-Atomic gold, White Powder Gold, Manna or ORMEs is the sought after "nectar of the gods" as the Ancient Mayans would say.

The only caveat is that they were looking for a marker to identify cancerous growth; but nonetheless, it will be helpful in the end to bridge the gap between useful telomerase and non-useful telomerase. It is possible that they did not quite get the particles of Gold (AuNPs) to a small enough molecule. Maybe if they took it a step further and literally reduced the Gold (Au) to one atom in a high spin rate, they would have discovered that it is the "food" for the healthy, normal cells!

# 9 ELITE GATHER MANNA FROM THE POPULOUS

The Priest class known as the Kohathites transitioned into the banking priest class we know today as the Elites, Illuminati, or Cabal. This was done through the creation of the fractional banking system. After the Igigi, in Biblical and Sumerian times, gold was mined using people and little technology. Although it could have been mined by the Igigi using great technology, and it was most likely the case, the humans we have come to know as the Bible individuals did not have such technology. There also were not as many people to do the mining, so I would imagine the Annunaki, if they were going to leave this task to the humans, had to either do one of two things: 1. Introduce technology for the humans to use which would redouble their efforts; or 2. Create a system which would autonomously incentivize the humans to create their own technology and mine faster and more effectively.

I believe it was a combination of the two, but it is difficult to prove that the first one actually occurred since our government is so unforthcoming regarding the ET phenomenon. So here we have to use the evidence at hand. What do "they" say? If you want to find the truth all you have to do is "follow the money!" This is truly the case when understanding the simplicity and beauty of the system we have been introduced to, which has not only incentivized us into creating all forms of technology, but put us in endless pursuit of the yellow metal known as Gold.

One afternoon as I was pondering the conundrum we humans find ourselves in today, called the financial crisis; how did we get into this mess to begin with? It is all over the news and hard to hide from the idea that the housing market got us into this problem, or the bailouts got us here, or that frivolous middle-class spending and borrowing caused this terrible catastrophe. However, even though some of the above shows promise, I think they are only symptoms surfacing that are caused by a much larger disease. This disease is called fractional lending. It is not the borrower who causes the problem. They may choose to put themselves in debt and servitude to a higher power called a lender, but really it is not entirely the borrower who creates this problem just because he wants to borrow the money. The real problem is identified once you ask the question: "Where does the bank get its money from to lend to the borrower?" That is the million dollar question that opens up the paradox we find ourselves in today. It is a virus that was created back when greed took over the safe keeping of precious belongings and in our case, GOLD.

Hundreds of years ago depositors decided they were going to not only keep the gold of their customers in a giant box for safe keeping, they decided at some point to begin handing out certificates which denoted how much the customer kept in the central safe. We now call these safes banks or depositors. As the depositors became more and more greedy, someone decided to hand out certificates and begin to mathematically delineate a formula which showed how often or how likely someone was going to withdraw their gold from the bank. Once they figured this out they invented a "trick" that allowed them to hand out more money as a loan than they actually had at any moment within the bank. They were "banking" on the fact that certain depositors would not withdraw their gold within a certain time period and could "pretend" that they had gold, which was not actually in the safe. This was the birth of fractional lending. And fractional lending is exactly what has built up the Federal Reserve's monetary power and thus perceived gold "reserves." But the sad part about this is, we might find that The Federal Reserve might not even have any gold in its possession once we do finally get to see inside Fort Knox.

But either way the important thing to learn here is not how much gold the Fed actually has, but that they do collect it and send it to its parent corporations and them to theirs. It is a giant Ponzi scheme, which most of us know is going on, but don't truly understand why. It is because it is the technology we either were inspired to create by the "gods" or it was given to us by the gods in order to gather the gold and centralize it. It is in mass centralization that the Annunaki can very easily control, collect and use at their whim. And all of this gets easier and easier for them to do outside of prying eyes the longer it goes on and the more centralized it gets. In the end, if this system is left to its own devises and survives, which as of this writing is showing many cracks and may not survive much longer, it will be so autonomous and centralized that all the Annunaki would have to do is send one being periodically to pick up the gold from one wealthy individual who has subsequently purchased a majority of the gold from the entire Earth. Does this sound far-fetched or impossible? Just look how easy it is to purchase anything anywhere in the world at any moment as long as you have enough money. You can even do it anonymously now! I would suspect that in order to fulfill ancient prophecy, the only thing left to do is to implant or tattoo identifying banking information on our hands or heads and the deal is done. Then it wouldn't take much to completely wipe out the bank accounts of all on Earth with the push of a button. It could even be disguised as a computer virus that would end up disabling the entire banking grid and rob the checking and savings accounts of all unsuspecting depositors on the planet. Of course, there would be no way for the average person to avoid this scenario because the Elite would force everyone to participate through a tax collecting levy or seizure if you chose not to comply. We all know how easy it is to go against the IRS don't we? It may not transpire using this specific strategy, but rest assured if anything in this book is true, the desire of the Elite to take control of your ability to buy or sell is in the forefront of their plans. As long as we have electricity and the Internet, it is more than viable.

So who are these people, we assume are human, who have been plotting the centralization of barter and trade for thousands of years? Who are the people which plan to grab as much gold as they can as our "Heavenly Father" approaches and intend to transfer possession? S. Jason Cunningham eloquently lays this identification on the table for all to see, in her book, *Smoke and Mirrors*, starting with the Original Tribes which entered the Promised Land:

> The most common interpretation is that Jesus came from the bloodline of King David. In fact the Bible tells us that it is Joseph who holds the direct bloodline to King David, although the bible later attempts to assert that Mary does as well. Should you believe that Mary is Jesus's true mother and birthed him in a Virgin birth, then Jesus does not have Joseph's bloodline, nor the more powerful direct line to King David. King David lived on earth roughly 1,000 years before Jesus was born. You can imagine how many thousands of people, at that time, had some claim to the bloodline of King David. So what would have made Jesus so special and why would the Romans have gone to such great lengths to obscure the truth? I think now the 'smoke' starts to clear and we now begin to see glimmers of the truth…
>
> …The Merovingian Line of Kings is the bloodline, which European Monarchies and many elite families in the western world claim. The first Merovingian King is believed to be a person named Merovech. As legend states, Merovech was the son of two fathers, one named Clodio and the other a mysterious 'creature' from across the sea.

Merovech (or Merovee) comes from "of the sea". As will be explained, I believe this is a representation of the

Tribes of both Judah and Dan, which both came from the Holy Land to cross the sea to Europe – "of the sea". It was Clodio, King of Salian Franks who lived in 426-447AD who was the father of Merovech (447 – 456AD)...

...It is believed that there were 6 Hebrew tribes, which fled and sailed to Europe. These were the Tribes mentioned as "of the sea". They were known as brutal warriors who named themselves after their perceived ancestors 'The Six Hyksos Kings'. It was these men who were renamed in the annals of European history as the "Vikings", meaning VI Kings for Six Hyksos Kings. One of the larger tribes of Israel at the time was Dan whose people were known as ruthless seafaring pirates. They incorporated the name of DAN, DEN, DON and DUN along their conquests through Europe, such as River DANube, MaceDONia, DENmark (which means The Mark of Dan), and even painted red and white stripes on their sails as the Vikings.

From J.H. Allen's book, "Judah's Sceptre and Joseph's Birthright"; "There is no grander theme upon the scrolls of history than the story of this struggle of the Anglo-Saxons westward. The very streams of Europe mark their resting places, and in the root of nearly all their ancient names (Dan, or Don) recall the sacred stream Jordan river of rest— from whose hands, so far away, as exiles, they set out. It was either the little colony of Dan, obeying its tribal proclivity for naming everything it captured (Jud. 18:1-29) after their father, or else the mere survival of a word and custom; but, none-the-less, it serves to TRACE these wanderers LIKE A TRAIL. Hence the Dan-ube, the Dan-ieper, the Dan-iester, the Dan-au,the Daci and Davi, the Dan, the Don, the U-Don, the Eri-don, and the THOUSAND OTHER dans and dons of ancient and early geography,

down to the Danes in Dan-emerke, or 'Dan's last resting place."

Many historians put forward the argument, rooted in historical record, that it was the Tribe of Dan that seeded the European Monarchies and its elite families. This is the bloodline of many of the modern day wealthy and elite families in secret societies, which I will discuss further in the book. What is the significance of the Tribe of Dan? Why should this concern anyone? I came across an article entitled "The Lost Tribe of Dan; The Early Jewish and Christian View of the Identity of the Antichrist by Janet Moser". In fact while I was writing this book, this article came to me in a dream. The next morning I looked it up and found it immediately:

As Mrs. Moser writes, "...Several obscure prophecies in the Bible point to the fact that the tribe of Dan will produce the Antichrist... From the carcass of the young lion [Judaism] the tribe of Dan will attempt to produce a golden age. The conspiracy of the tribe of Dan, aka the Synagogue of Satan, is to steal the messianic birthright from the tribe of Judah and establish a false messianic kingdom in Israel... I believe that the Biblical admonition to bless the descendants of Abraham [Gen. 12:3] includes exposing the identity of the man of sin who will lead many Jews to their destruction.

"The Merovingian's, who plan to rule the world from their future throne at Jerusalem, claim to come from the tribe of Judah through Jesus Christ and Mary Magdalene. However, the weight of evidence indicates that they descended from the tribe of Dan..."Samson the superman hero came from the Tribe of Dan but his mother was from Judah. Samson, in some respects, was considered a forerunner of the Messiah who will come from Judah but his mother, according to the Midrash will be of the Tribe of Dan." [Brit-Am Israel, 2/9/99] "I believe there is evidence to suggest that the False Prophet, a Merovingian, will rise to prominence and power as the Antichrist's right hand man."

"...Irenaeus also relates the coming of Antichrist to the tribe of Dan. He declares: "And Jeremiah does not merely point out his sudden coming, but he even indicates the tribe from which he shall come, where he says, 'We shall hear the voice of his swift horses from DAN...The Merovingians are the offspring of the tribe of Dan, which intermarried with the Canaanite Tuatha De Danann, also known as the Dragon Lords of Anu [as in Enki and Enlil's Father]. When God dispersed the northern tribes of Israel for their wickedness, the tribe of Dan migrated to Greece, and later to France and the British Isles where they established pagan priesthoods and royal dynasties of the demonic bloodline."

Another example of historians who follow the same historical truths is found in the book *"The Second Messiah"*, in which authors Christopher Knight and Robert Lomas identify the Merovingian families which conspired with the Merovingian pope, as a "Jewish fifth column within the Catholic Church to recapture the Holy Land: The picture that was emerging was of a group of European noble families, descended from the Jewish lines of the Tribe of Dan, who had escaped from Jerusalem shortly before, or possible even just after, the fall of the Temple. They had passed down the knowledge of the artifacts concealed within the Temple to a chosen son...of each family. Some of the families involved were the Counts of Champagne, Lords of Gisors, Lords of Payen, Counts of Fontaine, Counts of Anjou, de Bouillon, St. Clairs of Roslin,

Brienne, Joinville, Chaumont, St Clair de Gisor, St Clair de Neg and the Hapsburgs... By 1095, the members of the Rex Deus families group were almost certainly fully Christianized, yet each of them must have had at least one male member who held the traditional history of their high born Jewish roots close to his heart. No doubt they saw themselves as 'super-Christians', descendants

of the very first Church, and privy to the greatest secret this side of heaven. They were a silent elite 'the kings of God".

As seen, many scholars of history have researched this topic and exposed historical fact surrounding the Merovingian families and their true bloodline. I will put forward evidence to suggest that these Royal dynasties formed a web of secret societies, which exist to this day. During the medieval period, it was through the dark forces of these brutal Monarchies that the pain and suffering of the masses spread and intensified. Even today, social, political and financial chaos is perpetuated by many of these dynastic families from centuries ago. Could these Merovingian families fulfill the biblical prophecy as the "right-hand of the Antichrist"? Will they be the "False-

Prophet", or simply have a strong affiliation to 'it'?

As the biblical Hebrew patriarch Jacob declared, "... Gather yourselves together, that I may tell you that which shall befall you in the last days." Genesis 49:1 "Dan shall judge his people, as one of the tribes of Israel. Dan shall be a serpent by the way, an adder in the path that biteth the horse heels, so that his rider shall fall backward. I have waited for thy salvation, O Lord." Genesis 49:16-18 [44]

So if the Merovingian bloodline is considered to be the a branch of the tree of Dan, then what posts do these families hold that can be of significance today? Who are they today and what level of power do they hold that may affect us now? Cunningham identifies whom the original tribes were, who gathered in the promised land, and thus dispersed to Europe and beyond.; Where does this trail end which finds the actual bankers and financial decision makers we face today who stare down the barrel at us and seek to collect what they believe is due to them? There are quite a few families in a position of power and control of money but few, if any, are as powerful and notorious as thede Rothschild family. We can trace their genealogy to the Merovingians of the Basque region of France and Spain and thus back to the tribe of Dan. David Icke identifies this in his work "Tales From the Time Loop" here:

> One of the key human-reptilian 'royal' bloodlines later became known as the Merovingians, who were known as sorcerers or "priest kings", just as the pharaohs were in Egypt [In Icke's works he uses the idea of a reptilian race of beings inplace of the name we use as Annunaki]. The Merovingians were the royal line of a people known as the Sicambrian Franks. Francio, who gave his name to the Franks and died in 11BC, claimed to be a descendent of Noah (Sumer). The Franks called themselves Newmage or "the People of the Covenant". The Egyptians also believed they were the chosen people and had a covenant with God, a theme transposed by post-Babylonian Levite scribes to the Egyptian 'Israelites'. But for 'God' read reptilian 'gods'. The Merovingians/Franks can also trace their bloodline from ancient Troy and the Trojan Wars, up through the Caucasus Mountains into what is now France, a land to which they gave their name.
>
> Once again the Caucasus, this bloodline melting pot, was involved. At one time the Sicambrian Franks settled in an area west of the Danube and were known as the

Scythians, whom the Romans called "the genuine ones" ('The Sidhe' MJ).

Legend says that Merovee, the founder of the Merovingians, who died in 458 AD, was seeded by a reptile [Annunaki] and this bloodline is related to every royal family in Europe and a stream of others in positions of influence and control. The founding names of the Mormon Church, Joseph Smith and Brigham Young were both Merovingian bloodline and that's why the Mormon-controlled state of Utah has a beehive at the center of its seal. The bee or beehive is an ancient symbol of the Merovingian bloodline, as is the fleur-de-lis, so beloved of British Merovingian royalty. The hive is the symbol of the queen bee, the Illuminati reptilian goddess at the heart of their symbolism, and it also relates to the 'hive' mentality of the Reptilians that they have been seeking to transfer to humans...

...The Merovingians were supposed to have died out long ago, but in reality only the name disappeared, until recently, and not the bloodline. The genetics continued with the King of the Franks called Charles, more famously known as Charlemagne, to whom 34 of the 43 US presidents and so many other key figures are related. He vastly extended the Frankish domains and ruled as Emperor of the West in the papal empire created and controlled by the bloodlines descending from the Roman Empire. These in turn, descended from the royal lines of the Sumer Empire, Babylon and Egypt, who descended from the Atlanteans, Lemurians and the hybrid interbreeding programmes [Enki and Enlil]. Charlemagne was a contemporary of the Khazars.

The Priory of Sion ("Tsion" in Hebrew means mountain or desert monument - Zion) claims to be an elite secret society created in the twelfth century to serve the Merovingian bloodline or "Le Serpent Rouge" (the serpent blood). It says it was very closely connected to the Knights Templar who were officially formed at the French city of Troyes, named by the Sicambrian Franks (Merovingians) after their former home in Troy.

Prince Paris from the Trojan Wars stories also inspired the name of the French capital city. Another of the key figures in Illuminati genealogy is Alexander the Great, an ancestor of Charlemagne and all the major Illuminati families today. Alexander descended from the Viking peoples who settled the Mediterranean and the Aegean after the cataclysms and may well have become the white peoples of the region, including the Danites. Alexander ruled Troy at one stage and, before he died in Babylon in 323 BC at the age of 33, his army had seized control of an enormous region once ruled from Sumer. This included Egypt, Mesopotamia and into India. He founded the city of Alexandria in Egypt and, as he was known as the "Serpent's Son", Alexandria became the "City of the Serpent's Son".

Once again we see the recurring theme. The legend goes that Alexander's real father was the serpent god, Ammon [could be any of the "Annuna" or other sons of Anu], and this mirrors the story of Merovee, founder of the Merovingian dynasty, of whom a similar origin is given. The Merovingians have been linked with the bloodline of 'Jesus' by a number of books, not least those by Royal Court of the Dragon promoter, Sir Laurence Gardener. But the 'Jesus' connection isn't necessary to make the link between the "dragon bloodlines" of Egypt and Sumer and the Merovingians because they were transported to the Mediterranean region, Asia Minor /Turkey and elsewhere long before the era associated with 'Jesus'. The Illuminati are not going to have only one strand of the bloodline that is so important to them. The 'Jesus' bloodline is only code for the Babylonian/Serpent bloodline, anyway.

Throughout history, the Reptilians have perpetuated their 'purest' bloodlines by marrying as closely as possible to their own genetics and through the secret breeding programs. It is important to remember that these bloodlines do not just breed through their official partners. They have stunning numbers of children out of wedlock. These offspring are then brought up with names that are different to the major Illuminati families like Rockefeller and Rothschild. So when one of these children, called Clinton, Roosevelt or whoever, enters a position of power, the people do not relate them to the elite families because they have a different name. But, and I can't emphasize this enough, they are the same bloodline. This is how they hide the tribe, the reptilian genetic network. [45]

But regardless if they are attempting to hide some of the namesake, it is

117

quite easy to find a de Rothschild in a position or two of great power and control. In fact they are known to have amassed well into the hundreds of trillions of dollars in wealth over the centuries. This is a growing number as the gap between their wealth and the rest of the world's wealth increases. They are so aggressively building this wealth by funding wars and conflicts; bending the ears of central banks, and they even have the power to guide the price of gold. It is said that the Rothschilds alone tag the price of gold at the end of every trading day.

If these things bare true, then to what end do they take us? What is their goal if they want this power? They must have a strategy. No one with that much money and power arrives at that point through pure accident. There is always an overriding strategy to everything they do, whether it is to amass further wealth or even an entertaining holiday – nothing goes unsupervised and controlled. They cannot help themselves but to be in control of every situation they find themselves. So a plan must be in the wings.

Some say this plan consists of pure unadulterated domination and control over the peoples of Earth for amusement. This may be part of the picture. Although I am skeptical of this being the sole purpose of amassing such large quantities of money and assets, I am under the impression that the hierarchy does not stop with them as it never has. The hierarchy has always been there. And the want to preserve their lifespan has been more obsessive than the average person because they know that money must be made and protected so as to pass the goods up the chain.

What are the goods? Gold. The super-wealthy are gathering the gold. They are gathering this gold and have been for thousands of years under many systemic technologies to convince people to dig for it; to live for it; to want it and need it. The obsession may be genetically stamped. It may be suggested through Neuro-linguistic Programming. Whatever the case may be, we are taught to pursue this yellow metal. We are taught to trade for it. Why is this the case? Because no matter how high you go up the chain of monetary command: Boss, Owner, Government, IRS, Federal Reserve, Central Bank, Bank of International Settlements, Rothschilds, Enlil, Anu and so on, the goal is and always has been the same in human history - obtain more gold. Pass the gold to the Annunaki so that they can save their planet and live forever. We are slaves to gold. The sooner we can realize this truth, the sooner we can snap out of this hypnotized reality we find ourselves in called a global economy. There are more of us than there are of them.

It is written even in the Annunaki's own account of our history and their mission on Earth as they dictated it to the Sumerians - When the slaves rise up, the Annunaki take notice and change direction. In the case of the Igigi, our preceding slave race of more closely related DNA to

Annunaki, they all simultaneously raised hell and gold production came to a screeching halt. When the gold stopped flowing, the Annunaki listened. They created an alternative, called humans, to take their place and allowed the Igigi to go on their way. Now it very well could be the case that the Annunaki and the Elite have foreseen this uprising and this might be the reason for all the "wars and rumors of wars," but nonetheless we must push forward. As many conspiracy theorists have stated recently - they might be planning to create marshal law to tamp us down and restrain us from making much noise. They may cause power and communications disruptions or even government shutdowns (as we recently saw) as things start heating up within the "chatter" of revolution; they may plan on evil deeds, which could cause loss of life. But even if this looms on the horizon, we must not let it hypnotize us like a deer stuck in the unknown which he learns soon - is the beam of a truck headlight. It is our duty to survive. It is our duty to understand the truth and awaken to reality. It is our duty to strive and create the "city on the shining hill." Once we know the truth, we must speak the truth. Once we speak the truth we are heard. Once we are heard we begin the next step in our evolution.

Now it does not please me, nor should it please you, to foresee us being replaced by yet another slave race to mine for gold. However, what can happen if we do finally say, "enough is enough" is that something will be set in motion, by ourselves, for great change. It will be the greatest change our species has ever experienced. It will be in the form of a mass consciousness shift. It starts as a movement to extricate ourselves from the slave system, but from there we can decide who we want to be! The possibilities are endless.

So I ask you – WHO DO YOU WANT TO BE?

No one else should be allowed to answer this but you.

# NOTES

[1] Christopher Dunn, The Giza Power Plant: Technologies of Ancient Egypt (Inner Traditions Bear & Company, 1998). Kindle Edition. p. 191.

[2] Christopher Dunn, The Giza Power Plant: Technologies of Ancient Egypt (Inner Traditions Bear & Company, 1998). Kindle Edition. 192-193.

[3] Christopher Dunn, The Giza Power Plant: Technologies of Ancient Egypt (Inner Traditions Bear & Company, 1998). Kindle Edition. 193.

[4] Christopher Dunn, The Giza Power Plant: Technologies of Ancient Egypt (Inner Traditions Bear & Company, 1998). Kindle Edition. 194.

[5] Christopher Dunn, The Giza Power Plant: Technologies of Ancient Egypt (Inner Traditions Bear & Company, 1998). Kindle Edition. 195-196.

[6] Christopher Dunn, The Giza Power Plant: Technologies of Ancient Egypt (Inner Traditions Bear & Company, 1998). Kindle Edition. 196-197.

[7] Christopher Dunn, The Giza Power Plant: Technologies of Ancient Egypt (Inner Traditions Bear & Company, 1998). Kindle Edition. 197-200.

[8] Christopher Dunn, The Giza Power Plant: Technologies of Ancient Egypt (Inner Traditions Bear & Company, 1998). Kindle Edition. 200-202.

[9] Christopher Dunn, The Giza Power Plant: Technologies of Ancient Egypt (Inner Traditions Bear & Company, 1998). Kindle Edition. 203-205.

[10] Christopher Dunn, The Giza Power Plant: Technologies of Ancient Egypt (Inner Traditions Bear & Company, 1998). Kindle Edition. 205-206.

[11] Christopher Dunn, The Giza Power Plant: Technologies of Ancient Egypt (Inner Traditions Bear & Company, 1998). Kindle Edition. 207.

[12] Christopher Dunn, The Giza Power Plant: Technologies of Ancient Egypt (Inner Traditions Bear & Company, 1998). Kindle Edition. 210-212.

[13] Christopher Dunn, The Giza Power Plant: Technologies of Ancient Egypt (Inner Traditions Bear & Company, 1998). Kindle Edition. 213.

[14] http://www.gizapyramid.com/hidden.htm

[15] http://www.smith.edu/hsc/museum/ancient_inventions/battery2.html

[16] http://sentinelkennels.com/Research_Article_V41.html

[17] http://www.cheops.org/

[18] http://www.britannica.com/EBchecked/topic/237258/ggol-Au

[19] http://www.subtleenergies.com/ormus/tw/wgpowdew.htm

[20] http://www.youtube.com/watch?v=nm8IKtIhMnI

[21] http://www.openbible.info/topics/manna

[22] English Standard Version Bible. Exodus Ch. 32. Verses 1-35.

[23] David Clark, The Anunnaki of Nibiru: Mankind's Forgotten Creators, Enslavers, Destroyers, Saviors, and Hidden Architects of the New World Order (2013). Kindle Edition. 10-11.

[24] David Clark, The Anunnaki of Nibiru: Mankind's Forgotten Creators, Enslavers, Destroyers, Saviors, and Hidden Architects of the New World Order (2013). Kindle Edition. 14.

25 David Clark, The Anunnaki of Nibiru: Mankind's Forgotten Creators, Enslavers, Destroyers, Saviors, and Hidden Architects of the New World Order (2013). Kindle Edition. 15.

26 David Clark, The Anunnaki of Nibiru: Mankind's Forgotten Creators, Enslavers, Destroyers, Saviors, and Hidden Architects of the New World Order (2013). Kindle Edition. 17-18.

27 David Clark, The Anunnaki of Nibiru: Mankind's Forgotten Creators, Enslavers, Destroyers, Saviors, and Hidden Architects of the New World Order (2013). Kindle Edition. 21-22.

28 David Clark, The Anunnaki of Nibiru: Mankind's Forgotten Creators, Enslavers, Destroyers, Saviors, and Hidden Architects of the New World Order (2013). Kindle Edition. 19-20.

29 David Clark, The Anunnaki of Nibiru: Mankind's Forgotten Creators, Enslavers, Destroyers, Saviors, and Hidden Architects of the New World Order (2013). Kindle Edition. 20.

30 http://en.wikipedia.org/wiki/Showbread

31 http://www.shineonyoga.com/health-and-wellness-services-spiritual-anointing-with-young-living-biblical-oils/

32 Ginzberg, Legends, 2, 260; 3, 229–30, 287; 5, 396; I. Ḥasida, Ishei ha-Tanakh (1964), 37 (1964), 375. ADD. BIBLIOGRAPHY: S. Japhet, I & II Chronicles (1993), 143–62; B. Levine, Numbers 1–20 (AB; 1993), 171–75; W. Propp, ABD, 4:95–97.

33 http://www.subtleenergies.com/ormus/tw/shewbread.htm

34 http://ormes.wordpress.com/tag/alchemy-ormes-ormus-wpg-gold-stone-philosophers-m-state/

35 http://www.karenlyster.com/genesis5.html

36 http://upload.wikimedia.org/wikipedia/commons/7/74/ThutmosesIII-RaisingObelisks-Karnak.png

37 http://www.sermoncentral.com/sermons/christ-is-the-true-manna-jack-harris-sermon-on-divinity-of-christ-74105.asp?Page=2

38 English Standard Version Bible. John. Chapter 6. Verses 31-56.

39 http://ormes.wordpress.com/

40 http://www.subtleenergies.com/ormus/presentations/Dallas1.htm

41 http://learn.genetics.utah.edu/content/begin/traits/telomeres/

42 http://www.sciencedaily.com/releases/2013/03/130327133341.htm

43 http://www.ncbi.nlm.nih.gov/pubmed/20932008

44 S. Jason Cunningham, Smoke and Mirrors: Do Forces Exist Which Seek to Entrap Mankind in a False "Matrix" of Reality? (2012). eBook Edition. 38-45.

45 http://mara-gamiel.blogspot.com/2007/05/merovingian-bloodline.html

# ABOUT THE AUTHOR

Spencer Cross is a seeker of truth and pursuant of knowledge regarding the *currently* unseen. He is most recently a former real estate investor and after an unusual series of super-natural events during the year of 2012 decided to separate from his investments and refocus efforts to a more rewarding path. It is a path considered to be the path of Hope for humanity and the exposing of our true past and future.

Previously to this he was an entrepreneur in small businesses, a mortgage banker, an account executive at MBNA America and has a BS in Business Administration from Wesley College in Dover, DE.

Spencer is a family man with a wife, two girls and a boy. He will always be a surfer at heart. The life of the 5 year long Hawaiian waterman will never go extinct. Ever.

Printed in Great Britain
by Amazon.co.uk, Ltd.,
Marston Gate.